Courts and Criminal Justice

Perspectives in Criminal Justice 9

ABOUT THE SERIES

The Perspectives in Criminal Justice Series is designed to meet the research information needs of faculty, students, and professionals who are studying and working in the field of criminal justice. The *Series* will cover a wide variety of research approaches and issues related to criminal justice. The books are collections of articles not previously published, and each book will focus on specific themes, research topics, or controversial issues.

The articles selected for publication are revised versions of papers presented at the annual meetings of the Academy of Criminal Justice Sciences. Papers organized around a specific topic are reviewed by the book's editor and a panel of referees for comment and suggestions for revision. The *Series* will rely on a multidisciplinary approach to such topical areas as organizational theory and change, the nature of crime, law and social control, and applied research as well as the traditional areas of police, courts, corrections, and juvenile justice.

The current volumes include:

- *Corrections at the Crossroads: Designing Policy,* edited by Sherwood E. Zimmermann and Harold D. Miller
- *Race, Crime, and Criminal Justice,* edited by R. L. McNeely and Carl E. Pope
- *Coping with Imprisonment,* edited by Nicholette Parisi
- *Managing Police Work: Issues and Analysis,* edited by Jack R. Greene
- *Police at Work: Policy Issues and Analysis,* edited by Richard R. Bennett
- *Corporations as Criminals,* edited by Ellen Hochstedler
- *Juvenile Justice Policy: Analyzing Trends and Outcomes,* edited by Scott H. Decker
- *The Politics of Crime and Criminal Justice,* edited by Erika S. Fairchild and Vincent J. Webb
- *Courts and Criminal Justice: Emerging Issues,* edited by Susette M. Talarico

Comments and suggestions from our readers are encouraged and welcomed.

Series Editor
John A. Conley
Criminal Justice Program
University of Wisconsin—Milwaukee

Perspectives in Criminal Justice 9

Courts and Criminal Justice

Emerging Issues

Edited by

Susette M. Talarico

*Published in cooperation with
the Academy of Criminal Justice Sciences*

SAGE PUBLICATIONS Beverly Hills London New Delhi

For information address:

SAGE Publications, Inc.
275 South Beverly Drive
Beverly Hills, California 90212

SAGE Publications India Pvt. Ltd.
M-32 Market
Greater Kailash I
New Delhi 110 048 India

SAGE Publications Ltd
28 Banner Street
London EC1Y 8QE
England

Printed in the United States of America

Library of Congress Cataloging in Publication Data

Main entry under title:

Courts and criminal justice.

  (Perspectives in criminal justice ; 9)
  "The articles . . . are revised versions of papers
presented at the annual meetings of the Academy of
Criminal Justice Science"—
    1. Criminal courts—United States.   2. Criminal justice,
Administration of—United States.   I. Talarico, Susette M.
II. Academy of Criminal Justice Sciences.   III. Series.
KF9223.C69   1985   345.73′05   84-27755
ISBN 0-8039-2438-0   347.3055
ISBN 0-8039-2439-9 (pbk).

FIRST PRINTING

CONTENTS

Acknowledgments   7

I. WHAT SHOULD CRIMINAL COURTS DO?
Susette M. Talarico   9
1. Procedure Versus Consequences: Experimental Evidence of Preferences for Procedural and Distributive Justice
Anne M. Heinz   13
2. Two Thoughts on Plea Bargaining
Shannon McIntyre Jordan   35

II. EXPERT WITNESSES IN CRIMINAL COURTS
Susette M. Talarico   53
3. Determinants of Expert Witnesses' Opinions in Insanity Defense Cases
Robert J. Homant and Daniel B. Kennedy   57
4. Social Scientists in the Courtroom: The Frustrations of Two Expert Witnesses
Marc G. Gertz and Edmond J. True   81

III. COMPARISON OF DIFFERENT TYPES OF CRIMINAL COURTS
Susette M. Talarico   93
5. The Third System of Justice: Military Justice
Gary N. Keveles   95
6. Protecting Defendants' Rights: A Review of Literature on State and Federal Courts
Jack E. Call   121

IV. THE EFFECT OF COURT DECISIONS ON ADMINISTRATION OF CRIMINAL JUSTICE
Susette M. Talarico   137
7. Federal Court Impact on a Local Jail
Charles Weber, Albert C. Price, and Ellis Perlman   139
8. Contemporary Doctrines of Civil Death
George H. Cox, Jr., and David M. Speak   155

About the Authors   173

ι

For Rodger and Robert

ACKNOWLEDGMENTS

Several friends and colleagues assisted with this project. My sincere thanks to Loren P. Beth, Lief H. Carter, Joan Grafstein, Robert Grafstein, Margaret Herman, James Massey, Anthony Nemetz, Dean Rojek, Charles R. Swanson, and Terence P. Thornberry for reviewing the manuscripts. John A. Conley, series editor, provided considerable help at all stages of the project. Additionally, I am grateful to him for giving me the opportunity to edit this anthology. My husband, Rodger Carroll, guided me through the world of word processing, while our son, Robert David, took many a lengthy nap to see that we completed the project.

—Susette M. Talarico
University of Georgia

I.

What Should Criminal Courts Do?

What should criminal courts do? Although this might seem like a superfluous question, it cuts to the heart of criminal law and the competing demands that make its administration so vexatious. Basically, criminal courts function to maintain order in society. There are, however, a variety of factors that complicate this purpose: (1) the contradictory purposes ascribed for the criminal sanction; (2) the peculiar requirements of constitutional democracies; and (3) the competing demands that stem from a pluralistic rather than a homogeneous society.

As every student of criminal justice knows, there are basically four competing purposes ascribed for the criminal sanction: retribution, deterrence, incapacitation, and rehabilitation. The last three have a decidedly futuristic or preventive function; the first focuses exclusively on the offense and its punishment. Purposes for the criminal sanction are outlined explicitly or implicitly in criminal laws. Provision for type of sentences, alternatives to incarceration, and postconviction processes (probation and parole) assume some sanction goals. Outright endorsement of principles like restitution obviously reflects priorities also.

With the demise of the rehabilitative ethic, the move to determinancy in sentencing, and the emphasis on punishment and incapacitation, there is some agreement on the practical function of criminal law. And yet, anomalies persist. Indefinite sentences, rehabilitative institutions, and diversion programs co-exist with capital punishment provisions, restitution programs, and determinant sentences. These anomalies compound the already formidable tasks of criminal courts and complicate the jobs of prosecutors, defense attorneys, judges, and probation officers who struggle with the day-to-day realities of criminal law.

What makes this struggle even more problematic are the peculiar characteristics of constitutional democracies. In our governmental system, law not only seeks to maintain order but also to preserve the rights of individuals. It is impossible to achieve both completely, not to mention simultaneously. An emphasis on order sometimes requires that we partially disregard our concern for individual liberty. On the other hand, efforts to safeguard individual liberty frequently exact a price from society. The most efficient system of criminal law probably can be found in totalitarian governments where social order—however defined—takes precedence. The competing demands of order and liberty confront constitutional democracies and add to the burden of criminal courts.

Because individual liberty is probably never more seriously threatened than when the state intervenes to punish the criminally culpable, criminal courts have adopted stringent safeguards to protect individuals from arbitrary and unjust punishment. These safeguards typically take shape in procedural guarantees, and complicate the tensions already inherent in criminal court processes as the judiciary struggles with conflicting sanction purposes. If, for example, we recognize that an emphasis on due process regularity is the primary way courts protect individual liberty and if we recognize that rehabilitation requires individuals to defer to the expertise and particular judgment of authority, then it isn't hard to appreciate how constitutional democratic government adds to the already distressing burdens the courts carry.

It would be difficult to deal with the competing purposes ascribed to the criminal sanction and the contradictory aims inherent in our form of government in any circumstances. It is especially difficult in our pluralistic society in which a variety of religious traditions, ethnic and racial customs, and social and political perspectives abound. There is no dominant tradition in American society—save, perhaps, some sense of individualism and economic objective. Instead, individuals and groups espouse a diversity of preferences on how government should be structured, laws applied, schools run, churches supported, and families controlled. Because courts in general and criminal forums in particular function as a part of the broader social and political systems, there is no consensus that can be adhered to with any consistency or confidence. This lack of homogeneity obviously makes it more difficult for criminal courts to meet the varied objectives ascribed to criminal law and to balance the competing tenets of constitutional democracies.

The two chapters in this section speak to the broader question of what should criminal courts do. The authors' objectives and methods, however, are sharply divergent. In the first section Anne Heinz addresses a basic empirical question as she tests two alternative hypotheses about the expectations people have for criminal courts. Specifically, she asks if courts should focus on procedural justice—making sure everyone is treated in fair or regular fashion—or if they should simply ensure favorable outcomes—distributive justice. Heinz puts a normative question to court actors (defendants, victims, and police) in an effort to marshall empirical evidence. Given the fact that reform of criminal courts typically consists of procedural innovations (such as exclusion of illegally obtained evidence and the right to assert the privilege against self-incrimination), her finding that court participants have difficulty distinguishing preferences for procedural and distributive justice should prompt all of us to reevaluate the function of criminal courts and our prescriptions for reform.

In the second chapter Shannon Jordan looks at the practice of plea bargaining and offers a decidedly normative analysis. Explicitly basing her work on empirical assumptions, she speaks only to plea bargaining in cases having enough evidence to convict and when the court stands to gain from the waiver of trial, and offers an idealist evaluation of the appropriateness of the practice. Drawing on particular conceptions of social justice and ideal reasoning, she concludes that courts inappropriately allow plea bargaining. Although her conclusion only applies to peculiar circumstances, it should prompt considerable discussion on the manner and the function of criminal courts in our political system.

The Heinz and Jordan chapters illustrate the diverse methods that can be applied in the analysis of criminal courts and demonstrate the mix of normative and empirical issues central in any consideration of what criminal courts should be doing.

1.

PROCEDURE VERSUS CONSEQUENCES:
Experimental Evidence of
Preferences for Procedural
and Distributive Justice

Anne M. Heinz
Northwestern University

Miss Lavelle, smiling, said afterward that the verdict "strengthens my faith in the system, the American system, that it will work . . . I'd like to thank the judge and the jury for a very fair hearing"—interview after her acquittal in Federal District Court in a jury trial before Judge June L. Green on charges of contempt of Congress [N.Y. *Times,* July 23, 1983].

"This whole thing has been a nightmare . . . I'm very, very disappointed." Miss Rita Lavelle commenting on her sentencing on perjury charges before Judge June L. Green [N.Y. *Times,* January 10, 1984].

Recently there has been considerable attention in the social-psychological literature to the topic of procedural justice—focusing on the conceptual distinction between perceptions of the fairness of the procedures—and distributive justice—which addresses the fairness of the outcome. In keeping with the due process concerns in wide areas of legal decision making, attention has concentrated on the effects of

Author's Note: *The data were collected as part of an evaluation of the pretrial settlement conference project, prepared under grant 76-NI-99-0088 from the National Institute of Justice, United States Department of Justice. Points of view or opinions stated in this document are my own and do not necessarily represent the official position or policies of the United States Department of Justice. I wish to thank Robert Hayden, John P. Heinz, Wayne A. Kersetter, and Tom Tyler for their valuable comments and encouragement in the preparation of this chapter.*

different procedural conditions on preferences about court treatment and case outcomes. Such work has been used to propose changes in court procedure. It is argued that perceptions of fair procedures will help improve levels of support for the performance of legal institutions and, hence, attributions of legitimacy to the legal system (Thibaut and Walker, 1975; LaTour, 1978; Houlden, 1980; Tyler, 1984).

Such research asserts that perceptions of procedural and outcome fairness are independent. I argue that such an approach does not resolve problems of external validity and measurement, analytical strategies, and questions of research purpose. The concentration on procedural effects and perceptions of procedural fairness has obscured the significance of what is at stake, possibly coloring perceptions of the process. The stakes will, I propose, be more or less important, depending on the role of each participant and on the issues involved in the case. My analysis is based on data from a field experiment evaluating the effects of plea bargaining reforms in felony cases. By varying systematically the stakes of the case and the procedures used, I examine some alternative explanations of the ways in which participants evaluate their experience in the authoritative decision-making arena of felony courts.

The work addresses two issues in the procedural justice literature.

(1) External validity. Considerable work has been reported that is designed to determine what characteristics of decision-making procedures are perceived by participants to be more fair or satisfactory (Thibaut and Walker, 1975; LaTour, 1978; Walker et al., 1979; Houlden, 1980). Much of this research is based on laboratory experiments using college and law student subjects, with procedural variations carefully manipulated.

Such work raises two problems when applying the results to criminal court conditions. First, the subject populations do not represent the ranges of education, criminal career, or court experience that would apply to court participants. Further, the findings of role-related differences (Thibaut and Walker, 1975; Walker et al., 1979) among participants and observers suggest the importance of an additional refinement of the concept of participant to include the expectations of different participant groups—the defendants, victims, and police. Houlden (1980), using prison inmates and college students to rate case processing in hypothetical homicide cases, provides evidence that prior experience of the subjects shapes perceptions in significant ways.

Second, the more traditional laboratory studies have used as tasks the decision making involved in business decisions—and then inferred preferences about procedures in criminal courts (Thibaut and Walker, 1975; LaTour, 1978; Walker et al., 1979). The validity of that inference has been suggested but not fully tested. Houlden addresses the criminal courts more directly but uses hypothetical conditions and distilled case summaries. Therefore, we know relatively little about the extent to which different procedural configurations in the "real world" affect perceptions of fairness (Hayden and Anderson, 1980). There is some suggestion from surveys of defendants that perceptions of improved fairness may have more to do with individual presence at the decision-making process (Casper, 1978; Tyler, 1984) than with the structural relationships involved in adversarial or inquisitorial procedures, as Thibaut and Walker and their associates have argued.

Aside from the difficulties of transferring findings from the laboratory to the real world, there is an important measurement question about the empirical reliability of the distinction between the concepts of procedural and distributive justice. Although the conceptual distinction has been widely accepted, the tests, unfortunately, have been rather unenlightening.[1]

(2) Can procedural differences affect perceptions of procedural fairness independent of outcome effects? The research on procedural justice has concluded that procedural differences, *independent of the verdict,* explain differences in perceptions of satisfaction with the procedure. Much of the work has been directed at the policy issues of how to ensure system legitimacy in the face of the inevitability of some unfavorable decisions or outcomes. As a result, the research has often treated situation-specific information about the outcome as an unfortunate, confounding necessity that ought somehow to be removed from consideration. Perceptions of fairness reported after the outcome is known, for example, are interpreted as self-justification (Tyler, 1984; Reis and Gruzen, 1976; Houlden, 1980). LaTour (1978) notes that the two perceptions of outcome and procedural fairness are intertwined, and Walker et al. (1979) report reevaluation of some procedural preferences after outcome information become available. They do not, however, develop an integrated conceptual approach to interpret these findings.

A separate literature based on laboratory work includes evidence that the size of the reward available affects distribution decisions (Greenberg, 1978; Reis and Gruzen, 1976). In interview data there is some evidence that the severity of the outcome has direct effects on outcome satisfaction and even on perceptions of procedural fairness (Casper, 1978). Here perceptions of fairness are based on the calculations of costs and benefits rather than procedural issues (Reis and Gruzen, 1976). One implication of such findings is that the size of the penalties will affect the perceived fairness of the penalty and, in turn, the perceived fairness of the procedures.

But the linkage between outcome and process is not simply a matter of the chronological timing of the formation of each set of perceptions. The outcome presumably bears a systematic relation to the characteristics of the case at issue and may be predicted beforehand (Mather, 1979). I will argue that knowledge of the stakes involved in the case, including information such as the likely outcome and the costs of court appearances, will affect the satisfaction each participant attributes to the experience (Fetter, 1978).

This chapter, then, examines two perspectives on lay participant attitudes toward felony court experience—procedural justice at the magnitude of the stakes involved. It is predicted that those whose cases are processed in more open proceedings with greater opportunities to express their views will be more satisfied with their treatment and the outcome of their case. It is also predicted, however, that the nature of the stakes will affect their receptivity to issues of procedural justice.

DESIGN

Data to test the alternative perspectives come from structured interviews with defendants, victims, and police officers whose felony cases were part of a random sample selected in a field experiment to evaluate a procedural reform in plea bargaining in criminal courts. Included in the samples are respondents who did as well as those who did not know the outcome of their cases.

In order to evaluate the utility and limitations of the interview data, a brief description of the project is in order. The reform was designed to introduce the authority of the court into plea negotiations in what previously had been private discussions between defense and prosecuting attorneys, and to provide greater opportunities for lay participation (Morris, 1974; *Yale Law Journal,* 1972). These goals were to be accomplished by requiring that all negotiations about possible pleas take place with the judge present and that defendant, victim, and police officer be given the opportunity to attend any such proceedings. The reform was adopted by Dade County, Florida 11th Circuit (metropolitan Miami) in 1977.[2]

The evaluation was based on comparisons between almost 390 randomly assigned cases that were eligible for the pretrial settlement conference (the experimental treatment) and 450 randomly assigned control cases also drawn from the participating judges' calendars and from three additional judges who did not use the experimental procedure. Dade County had already instituted random assignment of cases to judges for its entire calendar, making the assignment at the time of arrest. As a result, the evaluation was based on random assignment of cases to judges as well as random assignment to treatment and control conditions. Participants were informed at the time of selection if their case was part of the treatment; those in the control sample were informed when the postdisposition interviews were arranged.[3]

The data for the evaluation consisted of observations of the plea negotiation sessions using the experimental procedure, and information from the court records for all cases and interviews. Structured interviews were conducted with defendants, victims, and police in the treated and control cases after the cases were closed; interviews were conducted by telephone unless the person was incarcerated, in which case, they were done in person (Skogan, 1981; Catlin and Murray, 1979).

Within this design are data for a natural experiment comparing the perceptions of those who did and did not know the outcome of their case. Although virtually all defendants were able to tell the interviewer the disposition of their case, approximately one-third of the victims and police were not aware of how their case had turned out. As a result, their responses may be compared to their fellow victims and police who were informed. Although no random assignment to the two knowledge conditions was used, there were no significant differences between those groups who did and did not know the outcome of their case in the average severity of their case, its outcome, or the way their case was processed.

Among those for whom staff were able to locate a telephone number or whom staff could find in a correctional facility, 54 percent of the defendants completed interviews, as did 78 percent of the victims and 63 percent of the police.[4] The interview response rate points out one of the difficulties of field research. The inferential problems created by imperfect response rates may be estimated by comparing the backgrounds of those who were and were not contacted. Comparisons of case characteristics of those interviewed and those not interviewed, as well as background characteristics of those who did and did not attend the pretrial settlement conference gave evidence of few systematic differences. Case severity, age, sex, race, education, and employment status did not differ between participants and nonparticipants (Kerstetter and Heinz, 1979). The mean severity of the offense and the sanctions did not differ among the three roles, suggesting that any self-selection bias in the interviews did not skew the original random distribution of cases.

The defendants, victims, and police differed in their background characteristics along predictable lines. Defendants were more likely to be male, black, and younger than victims. The background differences between the groups might be an alternative explanation for role differences in response patterns or attendence rates. However, when such differences were examined within the groups, race, sex, education, and job status had no effect on response patterns.[5] As a result, there is no evidence to suggest that the cross-group differences are a result of the different social positions of the groups. As will be proposed later, a more likely explanation lies in the nature of the court experience for the differing roles.[6]

MEASURES

The analysis builds on relationships between two perceptual measures of fairness that serve as alternative dependent variables and independent variables measuring case-processing characteristics and the magnitude of the stakes. Included below is a description of the construction of each and their values for the respondent samples.

Dependent Variables

The analysis uses two dependent variables measuring perceptions of the experiences of defendant, victim, and police. The first consists of an index of five items measuring *satisfaction with the procedure* used to dispose of their court case. The items dealt with the sensitivity or responsiveness of court personnel to the respondent's information and recommendations for disposition. Respondents used a scale anchored between very negative and very positive ratings.[7] Scores for the five items were added and then divided by the number of items answered to produce a mean score for the index that ranged from 1 to 5.[8] Defendants were the least satisfied (mean = 3.3), scoring near the midpoint on the scale. Victims (mean = 3.8) and police (4.1) were, on the average, satisfied with the way their case was handled.

Using similar procedures, a second index measuring *fairness of the outcome* was contrasted, using two items that asked about respondents' perceptions of satisfaction with and fairness of the outcome. All three groups averaged near the midpoint on the scales, suggesting modest support for the court's final disposition in their case. The mean score for defendants was 3.3; for victims, 3.2; and for police, 3.1.

The zero-order correlations between the two indices were .67 for defendants, .45 for victims, and .37 for police. The reliability of distinguishing between two such dimensions is examined in the factor analysis reported in the next section.

Independent Variables

Procedural effects. Method of disposition—This information was drawn from the court records after the case closed. Distinctions were made between cases that were disposed after a trial, settled prior to trial, or dismissed.[9] Because a case could be dismissed before or at trial, dismissals were included as a separate category. Settlement attempts may have been made in some cases that went to trial but no settled cases completed the full trial proceeding. Settlements occurred in 69 percent of the full random sample of cases, a rate similar to that for the cases of the defendant respondents (71 percent), victims (72 percent), and police (67 percent).

Treatment effects—A second procedural effect involves whether the respondent attended a pretrial settlement conference. Because the emphasis in this chapter is on attendence rather than the full set of possible treatment effects, the variable consists of a dichotomy between those who said they did and did not attend such a conference. Those who did not attend include those who were eligible but absent, as well as those who were in the control groups.

Magnitude of the stakes. The nature of the stakes is a way of conceptualizing the cost and benefit expectations within and among different categories of participants. I am proposing that the magnitude of the stakes depends both on the facts of the case and the different roles involved. From the work of Thibaut and Walker (1975) and their associates we have evidence of role-related differences in perceptions based on the degree of participation. Within the category of participant, however, there are other salient roles (defendant, victim, and police) structuring perceptions. I have deduced a rank-order in the size and salience of the stakes for the different roles. Defendants have the most at stake with the potential of prison terms. Victims have moderate stakes based on their victimization and potential of validation from the court disposition (Zemans, 1983). Finally, police have comparatively less at stake, recognizing that professional issues are their primary concern (Kerstetter, 1981). I have then used indirect confirmation by testing analagous within-role differences in stakes (the case severity measures) to see if they operate in ways similar to the hypothesized role differences. Although stakes may also vary depending on such factors as the amount of court experience or prior contacts among the parties or the publicity surrounding the events, here I am focusing on the case- and role-related aspects of stakes.

Two case-severity measures were developed, based on informal working predictions that could be communicated by the professionals/regulars to the lay participants:[10]

(1) Absolute severity—this index consists of the rank-ordered severity of the original charge, based on Uniform Crime Reports categories, and mutiplied by the rank-ordered severity of the sentence received (Diamond and Zeisel, 1975). It thus addresses what the actual exposure to the power of the criminal sanctions might be. As a way of reflecting the broad ranges provided in Florida statutes, the charge severity is included as a multiplicative effect. Among the interview samples, 30 percent of the defendants, 29 percent of the victims, and 27 percent of the police were reporting on violent crimes. As a point of reference for practices in the jurisdiction, defendants in 32 percent of the random sample of treated and control cases were sentenced to some incarceration beyond time already served. Of the defendants interviewed, 38 percent served some time. Defendants served time in 34 percent of the cases involving victim respondents and 30 percent of the police respondents. The index has a range of 1 to 12, increasing with greater severity. For example, a robbery (a violent crime) with a sentence of 10 years (above the average for the random sample) would receive a score of 12; a forgery (minor felony) with probation, 2. The mean for the respondent samples of defendants and victims was 5.0; for police it was 4.6.

(2) Proportional severity—This is a ratio of the severity of the sentence compared with the severity of the offense. It measures what might be termed the fairness or proportionality of the sentence, given the offense charge. It varies from less than expected (a less severe sentence than the charge, on average, might be expected to bring, compared to the severity of other charges) to more than expected (more severe than the severity of the original charges might be expected to bring). The proportional severity had a range of .30 (less than expected) to 4.0 (greater than expected). Examples of proportional severity (with scores of 1.0 to 1.5) would be a robbery with more than average prison time (1.3); burglary with probation (1.0); and forgery that was dismissed (1.0). Proportionately more severe cases (e.g., those with prior criminal records) would be burglary with more than average prison (2.0) or forgery with any jail time (3.0). Proportionately less severe

would be a robbery (.3) or a burglary that was dismissed (.5). The mean scores of 1.3 for defendants and 1.2 for victims and police show that the sentencing was, in general, proportional to the offense severity.

ANALYTICAL PROCEDURES

The first stage addresses the question of whether the perceptions of procedural and outcome fairness may be empirically distinguished. The tests for their independence involve the use of principal components analysis, similar to procedures reported by Thibaut and Walker (1975). The analysis was conducted on each of the three participant groups separately, consistent with the hypothesis that the groups would respond differently, given their varying stakes in the cases.

The second stage involves several steps. Alternative models, using procedural effects (measured by method of disposition and treatment exposure) and the case stakes (absolute and proportional case severity) to explain procedural and outcome preferences are examined. The work evaluates two alternative models. The first tests an operationalization of the procedural justice model: Procedural differences will be perceived as more or less fair that, in turn, will affect perceptions about the fairness of the outcome. The second tests the model of the costs and benefits—the magnitude of the stakes. In this formulation the size of the stakes will affect the perceptions of the fairness of the outcome, leading to a sense of satisfaction with the procedures. The initial analyses examine the perceptions of those who did not know the outcome; subsequent analyses are conducted with the perceptions of those who did know the outcome.[11]

In order to summarize the relative strength of the sets of procedural and case-severity variables, multiple regression equations were run twice, each time using hierarchical insertion of variables in order to make explicit tests of the hypothesized relationships (Tyler, 1984). To assess the procedural effects, the two procedural variables were entered after taking the stakes factors into account. The increase in total R^2 after their introduction indicates their contribution to the models of procedural and outcome fairness. To establish the importance of the stakes factors, the same approach was used, but this time the severity variables were added after the procedural effects had been introduced. The increase in R^2 may be interpreted as the amount of variance that is explained by the variable set in question, after taking account or independent of the effects of the other variables in the equation. These results are reported below the relevant tests in Tables 1.2 and 1.3 along with the total amount of variance explained by all the variables in the equation.

At each step in the analysis the results for the different respondent groups are presented separately as different tests of the hypotheses. I have posited that the three participant roles, defendant, victim, and police officer, may be ranked by the seriousness of the perceived consequences of the case.

FINDINGS

Dimensions of Fairness

Earlier work addressing the distinction between procedural and distributive justice has either relied on the face validity of individual items (Latour, 1978; Houlden, 1980; Tyler, 1984; Casper, 1978) or has reported considerable instability in the dimensions produced (Thibaut and Walker, 1975).

The results of the principal components analysis (replicating Thibaut and Walker's (1975) procedures as closely as possible) of the Dade County field experiment show that there was only one dimension that described the defendants' perceptions, but two for the victim and police. In each case the procedure provided for empirical rather than hypothetical specification of the number of dimensions to be selected. For both the victims and police, the first factor dealt with perceptions of outcome and the second dealt with the attentiveness of court personnel to the factual base of the case as defined by the respondent, consistent with the hypothesized distinction between procedural and distributive justice. For both groups, five of the six items in the analysis loaded on the hypothesized dimensions. The two factors explained a total of 66.2 percent of the variance in the victim responses and 68.1 percent for the police. The results suggest that for these two groups procedural and outcome satisfaction have different content, following the conceptual distinction proposed in the literature.

For the defendants there is quite a different situation. Their ratings of the ways in which their case was reviewed by the judge and their ratings of satisfaction with the disposition formed a single factor, explaining 62 percent of the variance. The most important variables in the factor were the outcome perceptions, though more than 50 percent of the variance in each variable was explained by the factor. These findings are especially important because they show that the distinction between procedural and distributive justice may not be assumed

TABLE 1.1 Principal Components Analysis of Perceptions of Justice

Groups	Factors I	II	Communality
DEFENDANTS			
(1) How fair was the outcome?	.89		.79
(2) How satisfied were you with the outcome?	.87		.76
(3) Deserved outcome severity[a]	−.89		.79
(4) How much attention did the judge give to your view of facts?	.71		.51
(5) How hard did the judge try to find out the facts?	.73		.53
Eigenvalue:	3.11		
VICTIMS			
(1) How fair was the outcome?	.87	.24	.81
(2) How satisfied were you with the outcome?	.84	.29	.79
(3) Deserved outcome severity[a]	.82	−.21	.72
(4) Were you treated better in court than other victims?	.00	.83	.69
(5) How much attention did the state attorney give to your view of the facts?	.16	.72	.55
(6) How hard did the judge try to find the facts?	.64	.08	.41
Eigenvalues:	2.71	1.26	
POLICE			
(1) How fair was the outcome?	.92	.14	.86
(2) How satisfied were you with the outcome?	.89	.10	.80
(3) Deserved outcome severity[a]	.80	.25	.71
(4) How much attention did the judge give to your view of facts?	.09	.86	.74
(5) How hard did the judge try to find the facts?	.29	.77	.67
(6) How much attention did the state attorney give to your outcome recommendation?	.51	.21	.30
Eigenvalues:	3.05	1.03	

NOTE: Selection of specific items from the pool made in order to minimize missing data problems and maximize fit of items to factor. Attorney performance questions were not given to defendants.
a. High score = more severe than deserved; for other items, high score = more satisfactory.

to exist for all raters. The attitude structures of the three roles suggest that the procedural and distributive dimensions of satisfaction or fairness are related differently, depending on the position one occupies. Consistent with the posited ordering of the three groups, the defendants—who were the most at risk—combined procedural and outcome perceptions.

Procedural Justice and
the Magnitude of the Stakes

Patterns among those who do not know the outcome. A natural experiment is available to assess whether the findings are only the result of self-serving judgments made in response to the actual outcome of the case. A large group of victims (n = 101; 36 percent of the total sample of victims) and police (n = 122; 32 percent) indicated that they did not know the outcome of their case and could not rate its fairness or their satisfaction with it. That information was not withheld, to our knowledge, on any systematic basis by the State Attorney's office or the court. Because that information was not randomly varied, inferences about its effect must be made with caution. Nevertheless, the groups of uninformed participants provide a useful opportunity to estimate the effects on perceptions of procedural differences and

TABLE 1.2   Evaluations of Procedural Justice and Stakes' Magnitude Hypotheses Among Those Who Did Not Know the Outcome of Their Case

	Perceptions of Procedural Fairness	
	Victim (N = 101)	*Police (N = 122)*
Experiential variables		
Procedural effects		
Method of disposition	–	.25*
Treatment	–	−.13
Stakes' Magnitude		
Absolute case severity	.24*	.27**
Proportional case severity	.11	.17
Proportion of variance explained (R^2)		
Procedure (after stakes)	.00	.06
Stakes (after procedure)	.07	.07
Total R^a	.07*	.09*

NOTE: Measures: Method of disposition: 1 = tried; 2 = settled; 3 = dismiss; Treatment: 1 = attend pretrial settlement conference; 2 = absent or in control groups; Absolute severity: case severity X sentence severity, range = 1-12, high score = more severe; Proportional severity: sentence severity/case severity, range = .3 to 4.0, high score = more severe than other cases; Procedural justice: index of perceived fairness of prodedures, range = 1–5; high score = more fair.

* = $p < .05$; ** = $p < .01$, *** = $p < .001$. Based on hierarchical multiple regression. Entries are standardized betas unless otherwise stated. Those that made a trivial contribution (F-ratio of standardized beta < 1.00) have been omitted. Proportion of variance explained measured contribution of variables after taking account of other variables in the equation.

magnitude of the stakes, uncontaminated by the effects of information about the actual outcome.

According to the model of procedural justice, we would expect that the procedural effects would be strengthened under circumstances in which the outcome was unknown (Houlden, 1980). If, however, case severity approximates the magnitude of the stakes involved, then those measures of stakes should play a significant role. Table 1.2 shows the effects of the two sets of variables on perceptions of the fairness of the treatment the respondents received. For the victims, who had been posited to have moderate stakes in the proceedings, the procedural effects did not appear at all. They explained no additional variance after taking account of the case severity. How their case was processed and whether they had attended a pretrial settlement conference made no difference in their perceptions about the adequacy with which the courts had heard their positions. Thus there is little to support the theory among this group of victims that the use of structured or unstructured plea bargaining or a trial significantly affected their views about the responsiveness of the court system.

In a second test of procedural effects, using the police, a different picture emerges. I had posited that police, having the lowest stakes, would be most open to procedural effects. The use of settlements (beta = .25, p < .03) and to a lesser extent, attendance at the pretrial settlement conference (beta = −.13, p < .15) made significant improvements (6 percent of the variance, independent of severity) in their perceptions of the fairness of their treatment. Thus, procedural effects emerged, and, as will be shown later, were stronger than they were for those who knew the outcome of their case. The direction of the preference was toward more open consultation but away from the adversarial model of a trial. Among the police, then, there was some support for the procedural justice hypotheses.[12]

The magnitude of the stakes involved—particularly the absolute severity—explained a significant amount of the difference in satisfaction with the way their case had been handled for both victims and police. In each case the two measures added 7 percent to the variance explained after taking the effects of procedural differences into account. It should be remembered that the information about the actual outcome was not available to these respondents. After taking account of the fact that trials might be saved for the most serious cases and therefore be a surrogate for case severity, case-severity measures themselves played a significant role in structuring respondent views about their treatment.

Why were victims and police in the most serious cases—who did not know the outcome of their case—more satisfied with their treatment than those in more minor cases? Victims did not have available the validation of their suffering, nor did police have justification for their hard work that might come with sentencing. An organizational explanation suggests that such victims and police in reality receive the greater attention and court resources that are devoted to serious cases—the "deviant" case (Mather, 1979). That increased concern has payoffs in terms of participant satisfaction. Alternatively, the court labeling of their case as more serious, as well as knowledge about sentencing practices, serve as validation of their predicament. To be labeled as a victim in a "minor" case where minimal sentences are probable and court attention is, perhaps, more routinized, would serve to denigrate their perceptions of their loss.

Procedural justice: procedural effects on procedural satisfaction among groups who knew the outcome. A more detailed analysis of the relationship between procedure and outcome and between experience and perception is available in the following analysis of respondents who knew the outcome of their case and were, therefore, able to give a more complete evaluation of their experience.

There was some limited support for the procedural justice propositions that different structures of court decision making affect levels of satisfaction with court treatment. However, the direction of effect was not always as predicted. The first test is found in step 1 in Table 1.3, which includes evidence of the procedural differences (method of disposition and attendance at the pretrial settlement conference) on perceptions of satisfaction with one's treatment in the courts. After controlling for the effects of degrees of case severity, 3 percent of the variance in procedural satisfaction for the victims and defendants and 1 percent for the police was explained by differences in the ways in which the cases were handled. For each group there were modest but consistent patterns.

Among the defendants the preference for trials or dismissals over settlements (f-ratio significance < .004) was important regardless of the magnitude of stakes involved. In addition, there were some nontrivial effects attributable to whether the defendant had attended a pretrial settlement conference at which judge and opposing attorneys were present and, perhaps, other lay parties. Defendants who attended such conferences were marginally more satisfied with their treatment than those who were absent or were in a control group (significance < .13).

TABLE 1.3 Evaluation of Procedural Justice and Stakes' Magnitude Among Those Who Knew the Outcome of Their Case

| | Satisfaction with Procedures | | | | | |
| | Step 1 | | | Step 2 | | |
	Defendant	Victim	Police	Defendant	Victim	Police
Experiential variables						
Procedural effects						
Method of disposition	-.12*	-.10	—	-.12**	-.12	—
Treatment	-.10	-.16*	-.11	—	-.12	-.06
Stakes' Magnitude						
Absolute case severity	-.28***	—	.16*	-.14**	-.09	.12*
Proportional severity	-.26***	.16*	—	-.16*	.13	—
Perceptual effect						
Outcome satisfaction	NA	NA	NA	.62***	.46***	.34***
Proportion of variance explained (R^2)						
Procedure (beyond stakes)	.03	.03	.01			
Stakes (beyond procedure)	.14	.03	.02			
Perception (beyond stakes + procedure)				.35	.18	.11
Total R^2	.15***	.07*	.04*	.50***	.25***	.15***

| | Satisfaction with Outcomes | | | | | |
| | Step 3 | | | Step 4 | | |
	Defendant	Victim	Police	Defendant	Victim	Police
Experiential variables						
Procedural effects						
Method of disposition	—	.08	-.08*	.07	.12	—
Treatment	-.09	—	-.15*	—	—	-.11
Stakes' Magnitude						
Absolute case severity	-.22***	.36***	.10	—	.33***	—
Proportional severity	-.16***	—	.09	—	—	.09
Perceptual effects						
Procedural satisfaction	NA	NA	NA	.67***	.43***	.34***
Proportion of variance explained (R^2)						
Procedure (beyond stakes)	.01	.01	.03			
Stakes (beyond procedure)	.07	.14	.02			
Perception (beyond stakes procedure)				.38	.17	.11
Total R^2	.09***	.14***	.06***	.47***	.31***	.17***

NOTE: Entries are standardized betas unless otherwise noted.
* $p < .05$; ** $p < .01$; *** $p < .001$.

Attendance at such conferences had even more of an impact on victims (P < .02) and police (P < .08) than it did for defendants. The other measure of procedural effects—method of disposition—made little difference in victim and police perceptions of procedural satisfaction.

As further evidence of the procedural justice model, the procedural effects should remain after introducing the perceptual dimension of outcome fairness. As shown in step 2 in Table 1.3, they did remain, although they still were modest. Specifically, the method of disposition remained as a significant element in the test among defendants (P < .01), added a small additional amount for the victims (P < .08), and remained insignificant for the police. Perceptions of the fairness of the outcome attenuated the effects of attending the pretrial settlement conference, although they did not entirely disappear, based on the somewhat smaller betas in step 2 than step 1 (and its disappearance from the model for the defendants). This pattern suggests that outcome fairness serves as one prism through which the responsiveness and structure of the court procedures are interpreted.[13]

Procedural justice: procedural satisfaction as a predictor of outcome satisfaction. The final test of the procedural justice hypotheses is to see if the perceptions of satisfaction with the procedures served to structure the perceptions of the fairness of the outcome itself (step 4). Noting the large betas for each group (.67, p < .001 for defendants; .43, p < .001 for victims; and .34, p < .001 for police), one may conclude that there is a strong relationship between levels of satisfaction with the treatment given in a case and the satisfaction attributed to the outcome. On the surface, the findings suggest strong support for the procedural justice hypotheses: The level of personal involvement in the presentation of the case is a basis for satisfaction with one's treatment that in turn structures the sense of fairness of the outcome. The findings for the defendants are similar to those reported by Tyler (1984) in his study of misdemeanor and traffic court defendants, although I suggest that the concepts are unidimensional for defendants. The strength of the relationship was considerably stronger for the defendants than for victims or police. My proposal is that the difference among the groups may be explained by the relative magnitude of the stakes involved for the different roles.

Putting the findings for the different groups of participants together, there appears to be some modest effect attributable to the different kinds of court decision-making structures used to dispose of cases independent of the seriousness of the charges or likely outcome. The directions of the effects were not consistent across the groups or with the procedural preferences for adversarial proceedings that have been described elsewhere. There is, nevertheless, some support for the idea that greater openness and structure in the proceedings and an opportunity to be heard was preferred. That proceeding was not tantamount to the adversarial procedures of a trial. Instead, it was, by and large, a judge-directed presentation of basic outlines of the case and agreement on recommended disposition (see Kerstetter and Heinz, 1979, for more detailed discussion).

Magnitude of the stakes: a predictor of outcome fairness. According to the hypothesis about stakes in the case, the magnitude and direction of the effect on fairness perceptions is determined by role- and case-related severity factors. Thus the severity factors would be most important for defendants and least important for police, due to the posited role-related variations in the significance or salience of the case costs. Aside from the magnitude, the direction of the effect would also vary by role: For defendants, the outcome of cases involving higher stakes would be viewed as less fair; for victims and police, they would be viewed as more fair. Conversely, defendants with low stakes would be more satisfied; however, victims and defendants in such cases would be less satisfied. This hypothesis is plausible if the outcome per se is less salient as the stakes are lowered or if retribution is an important goal.

The first step in examining the relationship between the magnitude of the stakes and perceptions of the fairness of the outcome is shown in step 3 of Table 1.3. The severity measures explain 7 percent of the variance for defendants, 14 percent for victims, and 2 percent for the police in their perceptions of the fairness of the outcome. The issue was thus less salient for the police than for the other groups, consistent with the hypothesized ordering of magnitude of the stakes among the different roles. Similarly, the importance of the stakes for victims and defendants (although not the order of magnitude between the two groups) supports the hypothesized pattern.

The direction of the effect differed among the three groups. Among the defendants, those with the most at stake—both absolutely and proportionally—were the least satisfied with the outcome and felt it most unfair. Among the victims, outcomes involving higher absolute severity (beta = .36), but not proportional severity, were viewed more positively. Finally, for the police, increased proportional severity of the case was interpreted as more fair. Thus, where the sentences given were more severe than the comparative seriousness of the charge would predict, police were more satisfied.

Magnitude of the stakes: effects of outcome fairness on procedural satisfaction. Perceptions about the fairness of the outcome played a major part for defendants (beta = .62, p < .001), victims (beta = .46, p < .001), and police (beta = .34, p < .001) in explaining their satisfaction with the openness of the procedures used in their case (see Table 1.3, step 2). The procedural effects and case severity made some independent contributions, but their strength was reduced when the perceptual dimension was added.

The perceived fairness of the outcome served as a halo around the perceptions of the adequacy of the procedures used. Within all three groups the outcome fairness played a dominant role in the evaluations of procedures. For the defendants, both the absolute and proportional case severity (measures of the magnitude of the stakes) made significant contributions. For the victims and police the effects of case severity diminished with the introduction of the perceptual dimension, suggesting that they also considered outcome fairness an important criterion for evaluating the procedures.

The magnitude of the stakes and the associated perceptual dimension of outcome fairness make a major contribution toward explaining respondent satisfaction with their treatment by the courts. Similar patterns occurred for each of three groups of participants in felony court cases. Further, the pattern was consistent with the posited differences among the three groups in terms of their stakes in the outcome of the court proceedings: The model worked best for defendants, when stakes were posited to be highest, and it worked least well for police, when personal stakes were posited to be low (although not insignificant).

SUMMARY OF FINDINGS

(1) The structure of perceptions about court experience differed among the three groups. For the defendants, outcome and procedural measures formed a single factor. For victims and police, the measures formed two dimensions, dividing generally between perceptions of procedural and outcome fairness.

(2) Several tests of the importance of procedural differences on perceptions of fairness were made. There were some modest procedural effects on procedural satisfaction for defendants, victims, and police.

More open, formal proceedings were preferred to less open, secret proceedings. There was a preference for having one's views heard but that preference could be met in different kinds of procedural settings. Thus, there was inconsistent evidence about the preference for trials over plea negotiations. In addition, among the police there were some procedural effects on outcome satisfaction.

(3) The tests of the power of the magnitude of the stakes to shape perceptions of fairness included evaluation of attitudes among those with incomplete as well as complete information about the outcome of their cases. Among victims and police who did not know the outcome of their case, the measures of case costs—combining case and sentence severity—were important predictors of treatment. (Similar tests were unavailable for defendants.) They were similarly important for those who knew the case outcome. The findings suggest that the knowledge of the actual costs forms part of a continuum that includes knowledge of the potential costs or risks.

Among those who knew the outcome, victims and police whose cases involved higher stakes were more satisfied with the outcomes than those for whom the stakes were lower. This pattern occurred after controlling for the effects of procedural differences. On the other hand, defendants were more satisfied with the outcome when the stakes were lowest. The effects of the stakes involved were more important for defendants and victims than they were for police.

(4) For all groups, perceptions that the procedures had been fair and that their views had been heard were related to satisfaction with the outcome, controlling for procedural and outcome effects. The strength of the relationship declined, however, as the posited size of the stakes among groups declined. The converse of this relationship also held. For all groups, perceptions of the fairness of the outcome and treatment were strongly related.

NOTES

1. Thibaut and Walker (1975) report that their efforts to distinguish the concepts were successful, based on principal components analysis. However, their tables show unstable loadings across different tests and even variable numbers of factors. Further, there is a significant overlap between role ratings (e.g., judicial performance, lawyer skills) and procedural effects (opportunities for evidence presentation). In addition, much of the research has relied on single items rather than scaled indices to measure effects (Houlden, 1980; LaTour, 1978; Casper, 1978). Tyler, using single-item global assessments made by defendants of the fairness of the outcome and treatment, reports a correlation between the two of .77, the size of which would suggest considerable overlap. Such approaches avoid the fundamental issue of the reliability of the distinction between perceptions of procedural and distributive justice.

2. From Heinz and Kerstetter (1979). The "treatment" was used on a set of randomly assigned cases in three courtrooms whose judges had agreed to participate. The

procedure was used for nine months. Cases were assigned to the treatment condition at the time of arraignment (about 30 days after arrest and 15 days after the preliminary hearing). They were randomly selected by the research staff from the felony arraignment calendars for the three participating judges. At that time, the judge, attorneys, and lay participants were informed that their case had been selected for the treatment, the content and schedule of which was explained in a letter.

3. The case rather than the defendant was selected as the sampling unit as the court needed to provide the same opportunities for all defendants in multi-defendant cases. In such situations one defendant was randomly selected to represent the case in the analysis.

4. See Kerstetter and Heinz, 1979, for discussion of interpretation of response rates. For similar rates, see Casper (1978) and Tyler (1984).

5. For defendants, race (f-ratio p < .74), education (f-ratio p < .62), and employment status, after taking account of the seriousness of the stakes (f-ratio p < .31), had little power to explain satisfaction with the outcome. For procedural satisfaction, these variables were also weak: race (f-ratio p < .84), education (f-ratio p < .17), and employment status (f-ratio p < .21). Among victims, the patterns were similar, with the background variables contributing little. Similarly, Tyler (1984) found no evidence of background effects.

6. Courtroom assignments made no appreciable difference in perceptions in the interviewed samples. Defendant, victim, and police response rates were the same across the different judges. Differences between defendants, victims, and police may not be explained by different judicial styles.

7. "Don't know" responses were scored at the midpoint, so the final index runs from 1 (very dissatisfied) to 5 (very satisfied).

8. Missing responses were excluded from the calculation of the index.

9. The charge uses statutory definitions of offenses. The original charge has been used as a basis for assessing the potential risk faced by the parties. Given that the sample excluded capital cases as well as misdemeanors, three broad categories ranked by the severity of the possible sentence have been used: violent crimes (homicide, rape, robbery, and aggravated assault), property crimes (burglary, larceny, and larceny of a vehicle), drug offenses, and other crimes (e.g., weapons violations, forgery, gambling, and prostitution).

10. This assumes knowledge on the part of the attorneys about how the sentencing norms operated, and correspondence between community norms about appropriate criminal sanctions and judicial behavior (Myers and Talarico, 1983; Feeley, 1979). During the discussion of recommended sentences at the pretrial settlement conferences we noted that the adversarial parties were rarely far apart in the starting "offers," suggesting that they know within a rather narrow range what the sentence outcome would be.

11. In a field experiment it is not possible to assign randomly the severity of the outcome, or the verdict as is done in laboratory research (Thibaut and Walker, 1975). LaTour (1978) used only innocent-believing defendants so he assessed only outcome correspondence, not outcome severity. Tyler (1984) used ratings after the outcome was known and suggests that one problem with his design is that the ratings of the outcome fairness will be self-serving.

12. The small cell sizes for trial and conference conditions limit the generalizability of these findings.

13. When the effects of procedural differences on those who did and did not know the outcome of the case are compared, we find mixed results relative to the procedural

justice hypothesis that information about the outcome would minimize procedural effects. For the police there was some support for the hypothesis: Procedural effects accounted for 6 percent of the variance in procedural satisfaction among those lacking information, but only 1 percent for those who had it. However, for the victims, procedural effects explained none of the difference for those lacking information but 3 percent for those who had it. One explanation for the pattern is that obtaining information about the outcome is a measure of the ability of the procedures to perform satisfactorily for those who have had little experience with the court system (victims as compared to the police). As a result, obtaining the information may serve to highlight the differences in procedures.

REFERENCES

CATLIN, G. and S. MURRAY (1979) Report on Canadian Victimization Survey Methodological Pretests. Ottawa: Statistics Canada.

CASPER, J. D. (1978) "Having their day in court: defendant evaluations of the fairness of their treatment." Law and Society Review 12: 237-251.

DIAMOND, S. and H. ZEISEL (1975) "Sentencing councils: a study of sentence disparity and its reduction." University of Chicago Law Review 43: 109-149.

FEELEY, M. (1979) The Process is the Punishment: Handling Cases in a Lower Criminal Court. New York: Russell Sage Foundation.

FETTER, T. J. (ed.) (1978) State Courts: A Blueprint for the Future. Williamsburg, VA: National Center for State Courts.

GIBSON, J. L. (1981) "The role concept in judicial research." Law and Policy Quarterly 3: 291-311.

GREENBERG, J. (1978) "Effects of reward value and retaliative power on allocation decisions: justice, generosity, or greed?" Journal of Personality and Social Psychology 36: 367-379.

HAYDEN, F. M. and J. K. ANDERSON (1980) "Questions of validity and drawing conclusions from simulation studies in procedural justice: a comment." Law and Society Review 15: 293-303.

HEINZ, A. M. and W. A. KERSTETTER (1979) "Pretrial settlement conference: an evaluation of a reform in plea bargaining." Law and Society Review 13: 349-366.

HOULDEN, P. (1980) "Impact of procedural modifications on evaluations of plea bargaining." Law and Society Review 15: 267-291.

KERSTETTER, W. A. (1981) "Police participation in structured plea negotiations" Journal of Criminal Justice 9: 151-164.

———and A. M. HEINZ (1979) Pretrial Settlement Conference: An Evaluation. Washington, DC: Government Printing Office.

LaTOUR, S. (1978) "Determinants of participant and observer satisfaction with adversary and inquisitorial modes of adjudication." Journal of Personality and Social Psychology 36: 1531-1545.

MATHER, L. (1979) Plea Bargaining or Trial? The Process of Criminal Case Disposition. Lexington, MA: D. C. Heath.

McDONALD, W. (1976) [ed.] Criminal Justice and the Victim. Beverly Hills, CA: Sage.

MORRIS, N. (1974) The Future of Imprisonment. Chicago: University of Chicago Press.

MYERS, M. A. and S. TALARICO (1983) "Crime coverage and sentencing patterns."
Paper presented at the Law and Society Association Annual Meeting, Denver, CO.

REIS, H. T. and J. GRUZEN (1976) "On mediating equity, equality and self-interest:
the role of self-presentation in social exchange." Journal of Experimental and Social
Psychology 12: 487-503.

SARAT, A. (1977) "Studying American legal culture: assessment of survey evidence."
Law and Society Review 11: 427-488.

SKOGAN, W. G. (1981) Issues in the Measurement of Victimization. Washington,
DC: Department of Justice, Bureau of Justice Statistics.

THIBAUT, J. and L. WALKER (1975) Procedural Justice: A Psychological Analysis.
Hillsdale, NJ: Lawrence Erlbaum Associates.

TYLER, T. R. (1984) "The role of perceived injustice in defendants' evaluations of their
courtroom experience." Law and Society Review 18(1): 52-74.

WALKER, L. E., A. LIND, and J. THIBAUT (1979) "The relation between procedural and distributive justice." Virginia Law Review 65: 1401-1420.

Yale Law Journal (1972) "Note: restructuring the plea bargain." 82: 286-312.

ZEMANS, F. K. (1983) "Legal mobilization: the neglected role of the law in the political
system." American Political Science Association 77: 690-703.

2.

TWO THOUGHTS ON PLEA BARGAINING

Shannon McIntyre Jordan
George Mason University

Plea bargaining is a practice so thoroughly entrenched in our present legal system that it may be said to be an essential ingredient of American criminal courts. In this Chapter I examine the issue of plea bargaining from the perspective of a broad, ancient philosophical tradition. Legal reasoning in Western societies reaches back to ancient Greece. The Sophists argued that law was man-made; its practice and origin is the result of power and persuasion. However, Plato, Aristotle, and the Eleatic tradition argued that law expressed the results of reason exclusive of pragmatic self-interest: Law means harmony, order, and reason. This opposition in Greek thought about positive law continues to be a debating point in modern legal theory. Realists hold law and justice to be a result of arbitration between conflicting interests; "idealists" hold law to be the necessary expression of reason, of a higher, perhaps permanent order of justice.

I will consider the practice of plea bargaining in light of two dimensions of an *ideal* understanding of criminal justice within the American court system. I shall argue that plea bargaining both distorts the relationship between offense and punishment and makes "justice served" in a given case a matter of market value. I consider both of these characteristics of plea bargaining to be failures of the ideal of reason that I believe ought to be instantiated in our criminal justice system. My procedure will be first to define the practice of plea bargaining and to note its reasoned justification. Second, I shall show that criminal justice is one ideal expression of a society's ideal of social justice. Here it will become clear that a society's ideals of social and thus criminal justice serve as standards in practice. Finally, I shall point to the problematic or unsettling dimensions of plea bargaining. These critical reservations of the practice issue from an ideal reasoning concerning both social and criminal justice.

My chapter is not concerned with what is actually the case so much as with philosophical ideals; it therefore does not reflect any empirical claims. In fact, whatever empirical assumptions are operative within this chapter are precisely that: assumptions. I have deliberately prescinded from an *empirical* analysis in order to enhance the possibility of a *philosophical* analysis of meaning. In short, I have undertaken what recent philosophers call an *epoche*. For these reasons my conclusion will fall short of determining whether or not plea bargaining should be undertaken as a practice. Rather, I am seeking to explicate the *meaning of the practice* as measured against the *meaning of the ideal*.

THE PRACTICE AND JUSTIFICATION
OF PLEA BARGAINING

The term "plea bargaining" is commonly used to refer to a pretrial agreement in criminal court procedures between defense and prosecuting attorneys—agreed to by the court—in which the defense agrees to a plea of guilty in exchange for the prosecution's agreement to one of the following: a reduction of charges, a reduction of the number of charges, a reduction of sentence, or a stipulation of lower sentence. Of course, the agreement is subject to the check of the court. In this chapter I examine two concerns about plea bargaining, but inasmuch as the practice is varied and includes under this rubric numerous distinct practices, I shall limit my discussion to those situations in which (a) there is believed to be sufficient evidence to convict, and (b) the state stands to profit in some sense from the bargain.

Here we might ask why all the officers of the court agree to a plea bargain. Answering this requires that we distinguish the possible *motives* of the actual persons involved from the *reasons* plea bargaining might legitimately be permitted. The psychological states that affect individual choices are known as motives. It is important that these be distinguished from the philosophical justification that may be given as reason for an action, behavior, or practice. It seems plausible that everyone involved in the criminal justice system derives benefit from plea bargaining, and consequently, each has a motive for supporting the practice in general as well as in particular cases. In a matter as important as justice it seems that motives satisfied or personal interests served cannot justify a practice that thwarts procedural justice. A criminal justice system that promises effective and even-handed enforcement of the laws is not fulfilled by a pretrial agreement to reduce charge or sentence when there is sufficient evidence to bring the offender to trial on the greater, more correct charge.

The latter becomes more interesting, for there appear to be at least two reasons for legitimating the practice of plea bargaining. First, plea bargaining is sometimes justified as necessary in order to literally bargain with the offender for testimony against others who have been engaged in criminal activities but against whom the prosecution has insufficient evidence for trial and conviction. Those who have knowledge of crime are often themselves involved in criminal activities, and those who testify against certain criminals do so at their own considerable risk. Hence, it is difficult to secure their testimony, and offering them something to their advantage sometimes accomplishes this. Second, plea bargaining is sometimes justified on the grounds that it is better to be certain that the offender will be locked up, even for a reduced period of time, than to risk that he will be acquitted. This is not the simplistic and self-concerned motivation of the attorney who is seeking a conviction to polish his or her record, but rather it is the acknowledgment that it is the duty of the state to secure the conviction of offenders, coupled with the recognition that the jury system is risky—sometimes the guilty are acquitted for any of various reasons ranging from legal technicalities to popular sentiment. For this reason, it may seem appropriate to secure the conviction of the offender through plea bargaining.

In the context of this justification it is understood that the plea bargaining system is not entirely arbitrary. Theoretically there are two checks on the practice—one on either adversarial side of the process—which keep a kind of balance in the proceedings. Specifically, the motives of the state and the defense serve as checks on each other. Attorneys on either side may plea bargain to avoid the unpredictability of jury trials—jurors are alleged to be "unreliable" and judges "unpredictable." It is important, as emphasized earlier, that we retain the distinction between motives and reasons for plea bargaining. In this discussion, I do not focus on individual motives; I only examine the jurisprudential reasoning behind the practice of plea bargaining.

Before examining this reasoning, we need to clarify the practice under scrutiny by locating it within its appropriate systems of social and legal justice. In this article I set the practice of plea bargaining within the context of the society's quest for social justice, and seek to interpret it within the parameters of the broader concept of justice. This particular undertaking stops short of suggesting a remedy simply because the work itself is incomplete. A more inclusive endeavor would entail a thorough empirical analysis of the practice in terms of actual existing systems. In this discussion I focus on the *meaning* of the practice of plea bargaining, considered in terms of the *ideals* to which our society professedly aspires.

IDEALS OF SOCIAL AND CRIMINAL JUSTICE

Justice as a concept may be as elusive as justice as a state of affairs; yet we can specify in both substantive and procedural orders the term "justice." In this chapter, the substantive sense of justice refers to a social virtue. Justice may be said to characterize the relationships within a society, between its members. A just society provides for, and guarantees to its citizens, those values essential for their individual and collective wellbeing. Obviously, this sense of justice is dependent upon some prior notion of the nature, purpose, and meaning of human existence. Hence the values that the virtue of justice promotes will vary according to a society's presuppositions regarding human life. Furthermore, justice in the substantive sense is understood—in all but the rankest of dogmatic, hence tyrannical, societies—as an ideal state of affairs. Justice is a goal of a society or a goal taken as an ideal toward which society strives and against which it measures itself.

> Justice in this sense is a concept by far more subtle and indefinite than any that is yielded by mere obedience to a rule. It remains to some extent, when all is said and done, the synonym of an aspiration, a mood of exaltation, a yearning for what is fine or high [Brennan, 1927: 87].

Our concern in this chapter is with social justice as understood by American society. Although it may be difficult to find universal agreement for this specific notion, we can here summarize some of its least controversial elements. Americans traditionally consider a just society to be essentially characterized by freedom, equality, and security. We say that we have a just society because it is characterized by these qualities, and we say that we are working for a just society insofar as we are striving to secure these values for all our members.

As a procedure the term "justice" refers to the standards to which a society and its legal system adhere in the pursuit of social justice. "Justice" here denotes the procedures that a society adopts in dealing with its citizens. In American jurisprudence the doctrines of due process and equal protection have been understood as the essence of procedural justice. We assume that this is true because we take it for granted that our laws do protect and that if all are protected equally and are guaranteed due process then procedural justice will be served (Jenkins, 1980; 351).

Obviously social and legal justice are interdependent. The fundamental goals of a society are partially determinative of the procedures that the society structures for its legal system. And conversely, the legal system itself, through its practices, determines in large measure those values that the society will promote through law and those it will neglect. Therefore, procedural justice determines to some extent and is a means to achieve the substance of social justice.

The relationship between procedural or legal justice and ideal or social justice is crucial for understanding and evaluating plea bargaining, and bears further elucidation. In *The Social Order and the Limits of Law* (1980: 351), Iredell Jenkins argues that justice can be understood as the completion of the law; that is, "Justice represents the ideal form of the order man seeks to create both through law and through the whole complex of his social institutions." Jenkins further argues that social justice has four major goals: (1) the cultivation of human potentialities; (2) the establishment and control of authority; (3) the inculcation and acceptance of responsibility; and (4) the assurance of continuity within the social whole.

An adequate theory of justice can serve as an ideal, by reference to which we can reach a sound assessment of the ends we propose and the means we adopt in our social, political, and legal efforts. Jenkins claims that the four conditions he has described are the essential goals of a just society and that all rational people at all times and in all places would agree to this. Nevertheless, it is the case that the exact meaning and content given to these concepts would differ substantially according to circumstances, time, and place. That is, there would be legitimate and honest differences of opinion concerning what constitutes proper fulfillment of these conditions depending, at least partly, upon what the nature of humankind is understood to be, and the moral, physical, and cultural conditions of the society in question. Specifically, the natural conditions are partially determinative of the goals themselves, the ordering of these goals, and the means selected to pursue them.

One of the institutions that is brought into being by a people in their pursuit of social justice is a legal system. Law cannot be understood as one principle of order within a society. In its law a society announces one element of its content for the concept of social justice and the means by which it chooses to seek that justice. The law of

a society thereby becomes a limitation on the possibility of the achievement of social justice. Although this may sound like a disadvantage,
it is not. As an abstract ideal, justice has little meaning for a society.
Instantiated in a formal system, it becomes a dynamic force that is
a condition of the possibility of the achievement of social justice.

We find that plea bargaining is, in fact, a common and accepted
element of our criminal justice system, and yet the two concerns I examine with regard to this practice raise questions about its relationship to justice as an ideal. One might argue that plea bargaining is
a functional practice designed to accomplish certain goals such as those
mentioned above. However, within our criminal justice system this
practice does require justification in terms of the concept of justice
itself. In the criminal justice system the people are represented by both
the judge and the prosecuting attorney, both of whom are charged
with seeking justice. Even in our adversarial system the prosecuting
attorney is charged, not with seeking conviction, but rather with seeking
justice:

> The United States Attorney is the representative not of an ordinary
> party to a controversy, but of a sovereignty whose obligation to govern
> impartially is as compelling as its obligation to govern at all; and whose
> interest, therefore, in a criminal prosecution is not that it shall win
> a case, but that justice shall be done. As such, he is in a peculiar and
> very definite sense the servant of the law, the two fold aim of which
> is that guilt shall not escape or innocence suffer. He may prosecute
> with earnestness and vigor—indeed, he should do so. But, while he
> may strike hard blows, he is not at liberty to strike foul ones. It is
> as much his duty to refrain from improper methods calculated to pro-
> duce a wrongful conviction as it is to use every legitimate means to
> bring about a just one [Berger v. United States, 1978: 88].

Notice that the prosecuting attorney is understood as a servant of the
law whose obligation is to see that justice is done. Notice also that
his two-fold aim is that "guilt shall not escape or innocence suffer."
It will be appropriate then to examine the practice of plea bargaining
in terms of the concept of justice.

In summary, then, social justice is an ideal toward which a society
labors. Because it is an ideal, it is not to be expected that it will be
fully actualized in any society; yet as an ideal it will serve as a guide
for social self-understanding and as a standard against which society
can measure its progress. Within each society there will be, necessarily, a criminal justice system. Once again, the concept of criminal
justice itself is an ideal, and once again, as an ideal it is never fully

realized. Nevertheless, as an ideal our concept of criminal justice also serves as a guide for our self-understanding and as a standard against which we measure our practices and ourselves. Because ideals serve as both guides and standards, they are of the utmost importance on the very practical level: We understand the practical dimensions of our lives and our actions in terms of ideals. With these senses of justice we can begin to measure the practice of plea bargaining.

TWO CONCERNS

I have to concerns or reservations about the practice of plea bargaining: First, it disrupts the necessary proportionate relation between offense and punishment; second, criminal justice is established by market forces rather than a deliberate process of reason. It will be important to keep in mind precisely what is under scrutiny in this section. In the instances of plea bargaining that concern me, there is believed to be— by all parties concerned—sufficient evidence to secure conviction and hence punishment of the offender on specified charges that by statute carry certain penalties. However, for various reasons considered legitimate regardless of private motives, the state—the people as instanced by the prosecutor—agrees to ignore evidence for specific charges and punishment, and accepts a plea of guilty by the offender on lesser charges. Note that I address only reduction of charges in cases in which prosecution has sufficient evidence to charge for more serious offenses.

The practice of plea bargaining can demean the ideal of justice in that it thwarts the harmony of crime and punishment. In order to clarify my concern, it will be helpful to discuss briefly the common, shared understanding of criminal punishment within the American social and political systems. Even though it is not possible to encapsulate the many diverse and even contradictory views within the system, I propose to take the American system as given, pulling out the commonalities. In the American legal system it is commonly understood that criminal punishment is appropriate only in certain situations—when someone has committed a crime *and* when he or she has been convicted of *that* crime according to certain stipulated procedures. Punishment, then, hinges on an adjudication of guilt. If punishment is to be "true speech,"—expression of fact in legal rhetoric—at least these two conditions must obtain. (These are not all the conditions necessary for punishment in our criminal justice system, merely the relevant ones for our investigation.) The conjunction of these two conditions for punishment is understood to assure protection of the integrity of the individual by preventing unjustifiable punishment.

A legitimate procedural conviction may be established either by the defendant's plea of guilty or by a conviction finding following a resourceful defense in a fair trial. In either case, a procedural conviction is understood to establish guilt in the initial sense, namely, that the accused *did* commit the crime. It is the conjunction of these two, initial and procedural guilt, that suffices to justify punishment. However, in this conjunction of conditions for punishment, we encounter the distributive element of the ideal of criminal justice in our system. Proper distribution requires both that punishment be accorded only to those adjudged guilty according to the agreed upon and universally applied procedures, and further that there is an essential connection between guilt in the initial and procedural senses. In fact, this is why procedural guilt is reversed when guilt in the initial sense can be disproved (e.g., new evidence comes to light after conviction). This also explains why guilt in the initial sense is said not to warrant punishment in cases in which procedural guilt is found to be unfair (e.g., on appeal). Although some might attempt to justify punishment on utilitarian grounds—though fewer might even accept a utilitarian justification of the criminal justice system itself—the conjunction of these conditions is nevertheless required for punishment in this system.

In the American understanding of criminal justice there is also a retributive element. Punishment is here justified as a means of redressing the balance between offender and victim as well as between offender and society. That is, punishment is understood as a means of reestablishing the natural harmony between members of society that was voluntarily upset by the offender. In fact, it is commonly said that the moral order *requires* punishment of offenders. This is why it is often said of those who have served the appropriate punishment that "they have paid their debt to society."

Notice, however, that this is only said when the appropriate punishment has been served. This is essentially a moral claim. Obviously, even one who has not served an appropriate punishment had paid his or her *legal* debt to society. The legal debt is, as the realist knows, precisely what the judge has determined it to be. But for the idealist this is not so. Although it is the case that punishment is a legal sanction, it is nevertheless based on a moral insight. The insight in the common notion of retributive punishment is that when one has behaved criminally one owes both a moral and a legal debt to society, and further that these two ought to be commensurate. This aspect of the com-

mon notion of punishment is vividly illustrated by any discrepancy between the legal and moral degree of punishment. Plea bargaining
reduces the concept of punishment to a simple legal category, thereby
rendering it a strictly nonmoral category. This does, however, run contrary to the accepted notion of the function of punishment that carries a strong idealist thread. The reestablishment of harmony in society and this redressing of the balance between victim and offender are
understood to require that the punishment "fit the crime," as the
popular expression has it. The notion of appropriate punishment is
deeply implanted in our legal system, for it is an ideal toward which
we strive. The intuition of appropriate punishment finds legal expression in the constitutional proscription against cruel and unusual punishment as well as the legislative classification of crimes into felonies and
misdemeanors according to their degree of seriousness. These provisions exist to guarantee that offenders may not receive punishment in
excess of the gravity of the offense. Now, this very same intuition works
conversely: appropriate punishment calls for appropriate severity in
sentencing. In fact, this intuition has evoked in recent years a movement supporting determinant sentencing to redress what is perceived
as a lenient judiciary and parole boards. Determinant sentencing is seen
as one way of responding to the problem of discretion in judges and
parole boards when these decide that a criminal has in fact been
punished adequately. Those who support determinant sentencing believe,
rightly or not, that certain offenses should be punished with a certain
severity that has not always been forthcoming. In any case, a common understanding that functions in our criminal justice system is that
an offense of a certain degree be punished in no less, as well as no
more, a degree—otherwise, balance cannot be restored to the moral
universe. It should be understood that there is not necessarily a relationship between a retributivist theory of punishment and determinant
sentencing. Furthermore, the removal of the practice of plea bargaining would not require the elimination of differential sentencing, which
can still be accomplished at the discretion of the judge.

A fair conclusion from the foregoing discussion of the distributive
and retributive elements of criminal punishment may be summarized
as follows. Although punishment is the legally sanctioned deliberate
infliction of pain in the form of depriving property, liberty, or even
life, society justifies this prima facie wrong on the ground that it effects a restoration of an essential balance called justice and limits its
distribution to only those cases in which the offender is both guilty
of the offense in actual deed *and* has been adjudicated to be so according to the established procedures. In other words, criminal law and

its sanctioned punishment protects individual integrity through its distributive limitation and contributes to social harmony in its retributive restoration of balance. Hence, there is something right, apt, meet, or appropriate—something *just*—about punishing offenders. It is my contention here that the practice of plea bargaining violates both the distributive and retributive elements of criminal justice; hence it is contrary to the very justification of punishment.

In plea bargaining cases, the retributive balance between the offender and the victim and between the offender and society is not accomplished. The relationship between the offender and the offended is not set right. If Mr. A forcibly enters the home of Mr. and Mrs. B., physically abuses them, and removes their personal precious property, then his actions constitute certain crimes expressly considered grievous by society. Its legislation calls for a specified—or more exactly a specific range—of penalty that is considered appropriate. Now, suppose Mr. A agrees to plead guilty to one count of breaking and entering with a maximum penalty of six months incarceration and two years probation. Even with sufficient evidence, such as the testimony of Mr. and Mrs. B. and possession of the stolen property, the prosecution agrees to Mr. A's bargain because he agrees to provide testimony against the leaders of a burglary ring. Because it is A's first offense and the police are very anxious to break up this ring, the judge accepts the pretrial agreement.

The reasons for this plea-bargained case are certainly legitimated by practice; however, it does not accomplish the redress our common understanding seeks. Obviously the victims will experience the hiatus between the offense and the offender's punishment. Not as unhappily, but just as genuinely, the offender will experience the hiatus between his crime and its punishment. (See both Kant (1887) and Hegel (1942) for an understanding of respect for the moral person of the offender.) Moreover, what was in fact a crime of assault and robbery morally calling for severe penalty is legally sanctioned as the minor offense of breaking and entering. Although society at large may not directly experience the hiatus between crime and punishment in this case—indeed most people will not even know about it unless the case received extraordinary press coverage— the harmony society seeks through retribution does not occur. After all, society has said by its legislation that in order to restore the disruption of harmony by assault and robbery the offender should be punished at a certain level of severity that is far in excess of the punishment received for breaking and entering.

Suppose now that Mr. A was successful in striking his bargain because he agreed to testify against a ring of burglars who could then be held to account for 15 burglaries. It is important to understand that many would interpret this as an acceptable bargain because, they might argue, a greater social harmony has been established in bringing these other miscreants to task. That is, they might believe that social harmony is achieved because we have achieved a higher utility—we have accomplished a greater aggregate of punishment to wrong-doers. We have done so, however, by backing away from a socially and legally proclaimed ideal of justice. The socially proclaimed ideal is not to achieve the highest utility, nor is it to accomplish the greatest amount of punishment to wrong-doers. Rather, it is to seek justice in each situation. The law does not say that when one has behaved as Mr. A has one is guilty of robbery, except in those cases in which it is to the advantage of society to declare otherwise. In such a case a society would be saying that social justice is to be pursued through law only in those cases in which it is expedient to do so. And yet, as we have seen, law is one instrument for the pursuit of social justice. Law both expresses our understanding of what social justice comprises and also determines our possibility of achieving social justice. To define social harmony as simply social utility is to back away from this ideal of social justice as it was presented earlier.

Although it is less obvious and more difficult to demonstrate, the distributive aspect of punishment is also disturbed by the practice of plea bargaining. The distributive element of criminal justice requires that punishment be accorded to those judged guilty in the procedural sense and that guilt in the procedural sense must be consonant with initial guilt—the crime in the procedure is essentially connected with the actual crime if justice is to obtain. Recall that this sense of justice protects the criminal in that he or she cannot legitimately be procedurally convicted of a crime more serious than the actual crime committed. Conversely, if criminal justice is to obtain in the distributive sense, then procedural guilt should be consonant with actual guilt and the punishment for procedural guilt should be appropriate for actual guilt. In short, punishment should fit the crime (this does not entail that punishment cannot also be made to fit the offender; although that may sometimes be a consequence of plea bargaining, it is not the most effective way of achieving this correspondence), and the conviction should be for the crime actually committed. In a plea bargaining case such as the example above, Mr. A did commit the crimes of assault and robbery. But the officers of the court, speaking for the people (for society) agreed to call the crime something it was not: breaking and entering. Consequently, Mr. A is procedurally guilty of and punished for a crime other than the crime he committed. In the distributive sense of criminal justice, then, plea bargaining is subversive inasmuch as punishment is not distributed on the basis of the actual offense committed.

The criminal justice system is one element of law in a society, and law, as a principle of order for a society, is designed and intended to serve the ends of social justice. When we admit the legitimacy of a particular practice such as plea bargaining, we proclaim this practice to be in the service of the ends of criminal justice—hence law; hence social justice. Is this so in the case of plea bargaining? It will be helpful to return to the notion of social justice itself and examine some of the dimensions of plea bargaining we have discussed in light of those characteristics.

We have seen that in plea bargaining there is a discrepancy between what is proclaimed as a consequence of lawbreaking and what actually happens to certain offenders. The people proclaim in statutes and in practice that certain punishments are appropriate for certain offenses, yet in plea bargaining these punishments are not forthcoming. Furthermore, decisions as to the distribution of the prescribed punishments are made on an ad hoc basis. These decisions are not made in terms of some dimension of the crime itself, but rather in terms of what the offender has to offer society as leverage against his or her offense. One oddity that is particularly troublesome in this regard is the fact that the more involved a person is in criminal activities the more likely he or she will be able to plea bargain. Furthermore, we find that in plea bargaining the offender is not held responsible for the crime actually committed, but for the lesser offense or to a lesser degree so that the punishment is not proportionate to the offense. As a consequence, the balance of the moral order is not redressed, and harmony is not restored.

Let's examine these dimensions of plea bargaining in terms of the goals of social justice as outlined earlier. Law is a great teacher in a society; it is the public statement of the limitations of freedom; it is the proclamation of the intentions of the society to support and to forbid certain behaviors. As such, law cultivates the potential of the citizen as a teacher, as one who gives direction and sets parameters. But in plea bargaining there is a discrepancy between what is proclaimed as law and what actually occurs. Law proclaims that robbery, for example, is an offense of a certain degree carrying punishment of an equal degree; but in plea bargaining this intention of the law is subverted. What is taught is not that robbery is an offense that carries a certain penalty, but rather that robbery is an offense, and only if it is to our pragmatic advantage will we punish accordingly. In fact, then, this aspect of plea bargaining—that it permits a discrepancy between what is proclaimed and what is practiced—subverts the first goal of social justice: the cultivation of human potential. A society cannot cultivate the potential of its citizens by teaching that the limitation of freedom and the sanctions consequent upon violations thereof are dependent upon the bargaining circumstances of the offender. Nor can a society cultivate human potential effectively when it permits, even encourages, a discrepancy between what is proclaimed and what is practiced as criminal justice.

This same aspect of plea bargaining is also a subversion of the second goal of social justice: the establishment and control of authority. When authority is established on ground that shifts to accommodate immediate perceived needs, the citizenry experiences a corresponding lack of confidence in the government. And finally, the fourth element in social justice—the assurance of continuity within the social whole—is threatened when the harmony of the social unit is not restored, as is the case in plea bargaining when there is a discrepancy between a crime and its punishment.

There is another dimension of plea bargaining that threatens the establishment of social justice, and that is the fact that the offender is not held responsible for the crime committed and is not punished in the appropriate degree. This aspect of plea bargaining threatens the establishment of social justice in the first and third areas identified by Jenkins (1980). It is interesting that in plea bargaining society fails the offender in two dimensions. First, society fails to cultivate the offender's potentialities; second, society fails to hold him or her responsible and hence fails to inculcate responsibility in that person. Both of these indicate a glaring lack of respect for the moral person of the offender. Human potential is not cultivated, and responsibility is not inculcated by society ignoring the nature of the offense that has been committed, simply because society can secure an advantage to itself in its pragmatic calculations. Both of these aspects of social justice, in order to be successful, require that the offender to admit appropriate guilt and be held responsible for that guilt in the approprite degree. The procedures of our criminal justice system recognize this in establishing procedural guilt either by a guilty plea or through the verdict of a jury in cases in which the defendant does not admit his or her initial guilt. Society nevertheless has the responsibility of responding to the evidence and securing conviction and punishment. Failure to do so indicates a lack of respect for the moral person of the offender.

My second concern is that the practice of plea bargaining demeans the ideal of social and criminal justice by rendering justice a market value. Recall that in a plea bargained case—even when undertaken for the best reasons, such as to obtain evidence and testimony from the admitted offender—there is sufficient evidence to accuse, and probably convict. Yet the state chooses not to prosecute the offense as it is declared in the statutes; the state chooses not to seek distributive and retributive justice in this particular case. If we believe that our judicial processes issue true speech, this practice, as an element in those processes requires that the entire community—including victims and perpetrators of crime alike—recognize that justice has been served and that this speech is true.

The community, however, proclaims its position with regard to specific crimes in advance of particular cases. Regarding this proclamation by the community we should bear in mind two philosophical beliefs that are deeply rooted in both the history of Western thought concerning justice and in American theories of jurisprudence. First, from Plato and Aristotle to now, Western philosophical notions of justice—whether in theory of natural law or natural rights—include the idea of justice as a determinate harmony that flows from an independent order or prior proportion and harmony. In its advance proclamation the community reflects its understanding of this harmony or proportionate order. More pronounced in Plato is the notion of justice as restoration of harmony; Aristotle further ties harmony to the human condition by saying that equity is justice that goes beyond written law. Perhaps his greatest practical contribution to the concept of justice is Aristotle's caution to legislators to provide a margin of discretion for judges in order to soften the rigors of the impartiality of statutes. This Aristotelian doctrine is reflected in the Code Napoleon, the Austrian and Italian legal codes, and in English and American common law. The practice of judicial discretion reflects the community's awareness that a wide variety of actions are covered by a single statute, and yet these may not all be deserving of equal punishment. Judicial discretion is intended by its wisdom to take account of this discrepancy between actions of the same class. The second philosophical root holds that the statutes themselves are the result of a society's ideals of social harmony. Justice, then, is a value held by a specific society that has a certain content that is expressed in its statutes. A criminal code expresses the society's understanding of justice.

Because we have decided to permit the practice of plea bargaining as an element in our criminal justice system, it would be easy to conclude that it is a just practice. Indeed, there are reasons for including it as a permissible practice, as we have discussed above. However, plea bargaining circumvents the process in and through which a society commits itself to the realization of justice. Even though it is a permitted or tolerated practice, plea bargaining does not reflect justice as a value established by the process of social reasoning because it treats particular cases as problems or conflicts to be resolved by adversaries on the basis of their particular circumstances: How much can this offender tell us? What good will it do us? What's it worth? In plea bargaining the resolution of the problem may be satisfactory to all parties directly concerned—it may even improve social utility—but the value of justice rendered in such a case results from a bargain struck on the basis of individual or market circumstances and not from the deliberate reasoning of society concerning the nature of the offense and the appropriate social response required.

The practice of plea bargaining thus clearly implies that the value of justice is a function of market forces. The forces at work in any given transaction—the "invisible hand"—will fix a price or set a value for that transaction. Although this concept of value may have theoretical and normative reference in the economic sphere, it is a categorical mistake in reference to criminal justice. In other words, justice is not the same thing in economic transactions as it is in criminal proceedings—a point well argued in Walzer's *Spheres of Justice* (1983). We can measure the impropriety of rendering justice a market value by the four standards of justice outlined by Jenkins (1980).

If the cultivation of human potentialities is a major goal of social justice, then rendering criminal justice a market value marks a retreat from the goal. Society proclaims in advance its position with regard to specific actions by declaring them crimes of a certain kind. Legal statutes proclaim the power of the state will be brought to bear against offenders holding them liable for appropriate punishment. Although one element of our communal understanding is that the power of the state will not be arbitrarily exercised, another equally important element is the expectation that the state will in fact bring to bear its power against offenders. Because in plea bargaining the state does not put into practice the ideal norms society declares for itself, it is a social admission of defeat in praxis—a retreat from its own vision of justice as a human potential to be achieved through its judicial processes.

When the practice of criminal justice renders it a market value, it is a signal to the community that beliefs about justice must bow to the authority of expediency. The ideals of criminal justice are severed from the reality of the practice. If there is no basis for the value of justice other than market force, then beliefs and ideals have no authority. The reality of criminal justice is not written by reasoned pursuit of an ideal; rather the author of criminal justice is the "invisible hand" that, to paraphrase Omar Kayyam, "having writ moves on/nor all your cries, nor all your tears/will wash away one jot of it." This fatalistic resignation to the authority of practice does not render to society the free establishment and rational control of its authority.

Because plea bargaining renders justice a market value, it retards both the inculcation and acceptance of responsibility. When the state does not hold a miscreant responsible for all of, but only some or lesser of his or her actions, then it signals that offenders and potential offenders are responsible to go before the law with negotiating chips, with a product with which to bargain in order to establish the value of criminal justice in the particular case. The offender's actual deeds thus are without judicial meaning; rather his or her deeds have the value fixed by the plea bargaining process. Such practice does not further acceptance of responsibility for the deed within the context of social ideals for justice.

When justice becomes a market value it loosens its connection with the ideal of justice as that ideal obtains context within a society. In plea bargaining justice becomes the value of particular circumstances governed by expediency; but the ideal of justice holds it to be a permanent and immutable value, at least insofar as it is understood and striven for within a society. If the value of justice is fixed by market forces, then its stock will rise and fall along with those forces. The value of justice will undergo cycles of inflation and deflation along with market conditions. Oddly, and counterintuitively, the value of criminal justice will go down as criminal activity increases to the extent that society—and thus law enforcement officers—need to bargain with offenders to obtain their secrets. The more sophisticated the criminal, in other words, the less exacting of the ideal will be the criminal justice process. Such fluctuation in the value of justice in practice is hardly an assurance of continuity within the social whole.

CONCLUSION

This chapter has examined plea bargaining within the context of the ideals of social and criminal justice in order to better understand the full meaning of the practice. We have seen that the practice subverts these ideals in several ways, rendering them less attainable in at least two specific ways. First, plea bargaining disrupts the proportionality between criminal actions and punishments; second, plea bargaining renders justice a market value.

It is not clear to me that these two concerns categorically invalidate the practice of plea bargaining. It is clear, however, that these are important concerns that indicate that there are heavily negative dimensions to the practice of plea bargaining. Hence, if it ought not to be discontinued, plea bargaining ought, at the very least, to be practiced reluctantly and with grave misgivings because of the inherent ambiguity of the practice.

REFERENCES

BERGER v. UNITED STATES (1978) 295 U.S. 78 (1935).

BRENNAN, W. J. (1927) The Growth of Law. New Haven: Yale University Press.

HEGEL, G. W. (1942) Philosophy of Right (T. M. Knox, trans.). New York: Oxford University Press.

JENKINS, I. (1980) Social Order and the Limits of Law. Princeton, NJ: Princeton University Press.

KANT, I. (1887) Philosophy of Law (W. Hastie, trans.). New York: Oxfod Kelley.

STRAUSS, L. (1965) Natural Right and History. Chicago: University of Chicago Press.

WALZER, M. (1983) Spheres of Justice: A Defense of Pleuralism and Equality. New York: Basic Books.

II.

Expert Witnesses
in Criminal Courts

Expert witnesses figure in both criminal and civil trials. Their testimony in criminal cases, however, is apt to receive more attention. Two cases stand out as good examples: the trial of Wayne Williams for the murders of several young black children in Atlanta and the trial of John Hinckley for the attempted assassination of Ronald Reagan. In the Williams trial, expert witnesses testified on the fiber evidence offered by the prosecution. Specifically, they focused on the probability that certain pieces of clothing, rugs, and other materials associated with the victims could have been found on Williams and his property by chance. In this trial, the expert witnesses provided detailed, scientific estimates after extensive study of the materials in question. Williams was convicted of the murders of some of the young black children killed in Atlanta, largely on the strength of the so-called fiber evidence and the testimony of experts.

John Hinckley's attorneys pleaded insanity in his defense. Court deliberations focused on two points: (1) the determination of Hinckley's competence to stand trial and (2) the determination of his guilt or innocence. Because the jury had to make an assessment of Hinckley's frame of mind and psychological state to evaluate the defense's claim of insanity, expert witnesses were called to testify. Psychiatrists testified for both the defense and the prosecution, and Hinckley was eventually acquited by virtue of insanity.

The expert testimony in the Hinckley case garnered considerable attention and prompted much debate. Both the popular and academic presses were full of critiques of expert testimony in criminal trials, especially to the degree that such testimony was imprecise, ambiguous, contradictory, or vacillating. Admitting that the state of the law and the particulars of the case left the jury in the Hinckley case with no alternative but acquital, critics still professed disenchantment with the medical profession and the value of psychiatric testimony in criminal trials. This criticism, in turn, sparked considerable debate on the role of expert witnesses in criminal courts.

How do expert witnesses function in criminal courts? In spite of the recent controversy, there is not much consensus on the role that expert witnesses—especially scientists and members of the medical profession—should play. Questions related to sanction priorities, the elements of a crime, the appropriateness of the adversary model, and the tensions between law and science persist and make such queries inevitable.

Regarding sanction priorities, it is obvious that particular kinds of expert testimony carry considerable weight in different schemes. For example, the value of psychiatric testimony would appear to be greatest in a system geared toward rehabilitative ends. To some degree, then, consensus on the role and function of expert witnesses depends on some identification of primary or priority sanction purposes.

In a system oriented toward rehabilitation, considerable attention is directed to one element of a crime, namely the intent. In a strict retributive system in which notions of liability are narrowly and strictly defined, most of the system's attention is directed to the offense, or a determination of the act. How we answer the question of the role of expert witnesses in criminal trials depends, in part, on our focus with regard to the elements of a crime. Stringent definitions of liability that stem from simple conceptions of retribution leave little room for expert witnesses, save those who testify to the particulars of certain actions.

Expert witnesses function in criminal trials that are adversarial in character. The adversary model is based on the idea that fighting for victory is synonymous with searching for truth. Each side seeks to win and the process serves to establish or refute the allegations levied against the defendant. When expert witnesses are called to testify in criminal trials, they are frequently subject to grueling cross-examinations in which the qualifications of the expert and the veracity of his or her claims are called into question. The adversary model has come under considerable scrutiny, particularly as critics charge that truth does not always emerge, that manipulation and emotional appeals substitute for impartial presentation of evidence, and that the aims of justice are seldom realized. Many of the difficulties experienced by expert witnesses and much of the controversy surrounding their role in criminal cases hinges on assessments of the viability of the adversary model.

Questions on the appropriateness of the adversary model raise more general queries on the relationship between law and science. Is the scientific method compatible with the "truth-seeking" objectives of the adversary model? Are lawyers and scientists able to communicate in the same forum and to the same end? To what degree do nonscientific perspectives influence expert testimony? These questions are considered in the two chapters in this section. In their study of expert witnesses' opinions in insanity defense cases, Homant and Kennedy examine the degree to which personal, subjective preferences affect the attitudes of potential expert witnesses toward the insanity defense in general. Additionally, they ask a sample of potential expert witnesses for an assessment of a hypothetical court case. In this segment, Homant and Kennedy report on a study of expert witnesses' opinions.

In contrast to the Homant-Kennedy chapter, Gertz and True describe their experiences as expert witnesses in a criminal trial. In the case at hand a woman was charged with the murder of her husband. Claiming she was a victim of spouse abuse, her attorney argued the case using the battered wife syndrome, essentially a variant of a self-defense theme. Authorities were called by the defense to establish the woman's claims and to establish the scientific validity of the syndrome in question. Gertz and True testified for the prosecution. In particular, they were asked to evaluate the scientific credibility of the expert witnesses and the strength of their testimony on both the syndrome and the case at hand. Detailing their frustations with their experiences as expert witnesses, Gertz and True analyze the tensions between law and science. Like Homant and Kennedy, they call for a limited role for expert witnesses in criminal trials—a perspective that suggests that the basic tensions between law and science will continue to cloud both our expectations for and our evaluations of the role of such witnesses in criminal trials.

3.

DETERMINANTS OF EXPERT WITNESSES' OPINIONS IN INSANITY DEFENSE CASES

Robert J. Homant
Daniel B. Kennedy
University of Detroit

The insanity defense has come under renewed attack lately, both in the public and professional media. This attack has, in turn, motivated various defenses of the insanity defense. The research reported here explores the extent to which opinions about the insanity defense are a function of personal values rather than empirical evidence, and determines whether such opinions are likely to bias the testimony of expert witnesses.

For purposes of this research we have identified six global attitudes toward the insanity defense, labeled A through F. We do not maintain that there are no other possible positions, and we concede that one might wish to subdivide some of these (especially positions B and C) into two or more positions. But we do feel that this classification system is parsimonious, and that it is supported by a literature review of positions toward the insanity defense. We present the following positions in decreasing order of their acceptance of the insanity defense.

Position A: This position basically accepts the insanity defense with no significant objections. At least some serious criminal behavior is the result of mental illness (either a biological or psychological construct), and the courts are able to distinguish some of these individuals and to divert them into the mental health system, which is preferable to prison for some offenders. (May include minor objections.)

Position A is fairly close to mainstream psychiatric opinion, as expressed by the recent Insanity Defense Work Group (1983) of the American Psychiatric Association.

Position B: This position is not philosophically opposed to the insanity defense, but has some reservations in that society is unprotected. The harm to society may come from too broad a concept of insanity, providing an excuse for antisocial or irresponsible behavior, or from lack of control over those found not guilty by reason of insanity. It advocates reforms such as more restrictive definition of insanity, more burden of proof on the defense, mandatory confinement of the legally insane, and some guarantee against premature release from the state hospital system.

Position B is, in effect, a reform variation of A, usually given in response to a variety of criticisms of the insanity defense in practice. Ingram (1983) and Lockwood (1983) are recent advocates of this type of position.

Position C: Although this position is sympathetic to medical model thinking, it does not believe that courtroom testimony is very credible. There are a number of reasons that testimony may lack credibility: (1) psychological tests and interviews may lack postdictive validity; (2) the legal concept of insanity may correspond poorly with mental illness or psychosis; (3) offenders may deliberately fool experts; (4) lawyers may manipulate experts; and (5) experts may be biased for the side that hires them. This position might prefer that psychiatric testimony be given after the trial in order to aid in the sentencing decision only.

In a book often cited as the paradigm of medical model thinking in corrections, Menninger (1966) argues that because of the adversary system, psychiatric courtroom testimony is unreliable. Although he presents a comprehensive alternative approach, it is not clear what he would recommend if his choice were limited to a reform of the insanity defense, rather than an overhaul of the entire judicial and corrections process.

Position D: In this view, most crime is seen as a response to helplessness, or some form of socially induced maladjustment; thus the whole mechanism of determining guilt and blame is suspect. The insanity defense is seen as a device that allows the state to punish"sane" offenders with a clear conscience. It may be accepted as a necessary evil if the alternative is to punish all offenders.

This, too, is Menninger's (1966) view. Thus if Menninger's way of thinking were to be adopted, the insanity defense would be totally eliminated. In practice, however, an advocate of position D would be concerned lest abolition of insanity provide an excuse for punishing (rather than helping) all offenders. (For a similar style of argument, see also Monahan, 1973.)

Position E: This view objects to the characterization of crime as an illness. Rather it is a reasonable response to an unreasonable society. Although offenders may need support, concern, mediation, or skills training, there is nothing wrong with their psyches; the insanity defense is a device that allows the system to taint all offenders with the label of "unreasonable." When the defense is "successful," it also gives the system total control over the offender, allowing indefinite incarceration under the guise of treatment.

The clearest statement of position E is in Mark Morris (1976). In general, the objection is to the medical model itself, not because it excuses offenders (see MacNamara, 1977), but because it provides a rationale for increased state control.

Position F: This view—as does position E—also denies the reality of mental illness. Here, however, mental illness or insanity is a device that allows the offender to escape moral and legal responsibility. Even those who appear to be hopelessly insane are aware of their actions and in control of their behavior—hence deserving punishment. In mild form, position F may accept some concept of mental illness but believes the individual retains control, and therefore responsibility. F denies the relevance of mental illness to (most) criminal behavior.

Position F is essentially the position that has been defended by Thomas Szasz (1960; 1968).

POLITICAL-IDEOLOGICAL BASIS

Although it is most evident for position E, all of the above positions have political and ideological implications. Indeed, the political nature of the insanity defense has been evident throughout its legal development (see Christenson, 1983). In a historical study of American assassins, Clarke (1982) showed how the political system has walked a tightrope in order to avoid concluding on the one hand that assassins had a rational basis for their actions or, on the other hand, excusing them.

The ideological basis for one's position on social control issues has been analyzed by Stoll (1968). She maintained that one's preference for either punishment or rehabilitation was a function of beliefs about personal responsibility. She also distinguished between a psychiatric view, which favors sickness, and a psychological view of deviance as a "learned response."

Miller (1973) also maintains that there is a strong linkage between one's beliefs about responsibility and one's positions on a wide variety of criminal justice issues. Although the insanity defense is not directly involved in his analyis, the medical model—on which that defense depends—does figure prominently. Miller maintains that there are ten discrete but overlapping ideological positions that can be identified, five on each side of a neutral, middle-of-the-road position; however, this neutral point is not directly described. The two positions just to the left of center are the most sympathetic to the medical model and therefore, in our analysis, would be most likely to endorse position A. As one moves somewhat further to the left on Miller's continuum, however, crime begins to be seen as caused more by social conditions than by individual pathology. Separating out those who are legally insane and hence not responsible from the criminally responsible becomes a hopeless legal game (position C) or worse, a device to allow the state to punish "the guilty" with a clear conscience (position D). At the far left of Miller's continuum it is society, not the offender, that is seen as irrational (position E).

Conversely, as one moves to the right of Miller's continuum the concern begins to shift to security—to the need to protect society from both sane and insane offenders, although punishment is not appropriate for the insane (position B). As one reaches the extreme right of the continuum, the primary concern lies with holding all individuals responsible for all of their behavior (position F).

Research Problem

Our analysis of the ideological nature of positions on the insanity defense raises two separate questions. First, to what extent can attitudes in general be accounted for on the basis of ideology? Secondly, to what extent do generalized attitudes about insanity affect judgment of insanity in a particular case? Ideally, these questions would be dealt with in one global study, so that a direct link could be made between personal ideology and judgment in a particular case. We felt, however, that the amount of data that would be needed from each subject for such a global study would be too burdensome, and would result in a very low participation rate. Therefore, we decided to approach these questions as two separate studies.

STUDY 1: IDEOLOGY AND ATTITUDES TOWARD THE INSANITY DEFENSE

Subjects

The sample for Study 1 consisted of 200 clinical psychologists and 200 psychiatrists who were randomly sampled from the Detroit-area Yellow Pages. Complete returns were received from 57 psychologists and 55 psychiatrists. Although these two groups differed on a number of demographic characteristics (age, experience, gender, race), this did not significantly affect any of the results to be reported below.

The Questionnaire

Along with a cover letter and a stamped return envelope, subjects received a two-page questionnaire. On the first page, in addition to other demographic data, subjects were asked if they had ever been an expert witness in a criminal trial involving an insanity plea, and, if so, how often.

This question was followed by the principal measure of the dependent variable, the following 11-point graphic scale:

1	2	3	4	5	6	7	8	9	10	11
invalid					undecided					valid

Please use the above scale to indicate your position on the validity and usefulness of the insanity defense. (Circle one number.) Briefly, what is the main reason for your position on the above scale? [Subjects were given about three inches of space to respond to this open-ended question.]

The second page of the questionnaire contained 12 statements for which subjects were asked to give their degree of agreement-disagreement on a 5-point scale, in which 5 = strongly agree; 4 = agree; and so on. Six of these items (see Table 3.1, results section) were designed to elicit more specifics on attitudes toward the insanity defense. The remaining six items constituted a short-form version of the Locus of Responsibility for Crime (LRC) scale (Lillyquist, 1980: 59-66).

The LRC Scale

The major independent variable used for Study 1 is ideological position. Secondary independent variables are professional identity and expert witness. Ideological position is defined conceptually as a subject's position along Miller's continuum. This, in turn, can be measured by Lillyquist's (1980) LRC scale.

The LRC scale consists of 20 items whose content is derived from Miller's (1973) description of the various ideological positions. Two typical items (also used for our short form LRC) are:

> Criminal behavior is largely due to a lack of respect for basic moral principles; [reverse scored]
> Labeling a person "criminal" makes it more likely that he or she will be criminal.

The LRC scale is scored in Likert fashion, giving a total score that can range from 20 (conservative; right) to 100 (liberal; left), with a midpoint of 60. Mean total scores have been found to distinguish criminal justice majors from psychology majors (the latter score higher), and criminal justice majors from psychology majors (the latter score higher), and criminal justice majors with in-service field experience from those without (the latter score higher; Lillyquist, 1980).

The short-form version of the LRC was constructed especially for this research, and consists of 6 items taken directly from the LRC (items 1, 2, 6, 12, 14, and 19). The short form LRC provides scores ranging from 6 to 30, with 18 as the midpoint. Pilot work with the short form showed that it had a high correlation with the original LRC ($r = +.80$, df 52, $p < .001$).

Hypotheses

There are three specific hypotheses for this study:

H_1: Psychiatrists will be more favorable than psychologists in their attitudes toward the insanity defense.

The rationale for hypothesis 1 rests on the belief that compared to clinical psychology, psychiatric training is more compatible with a more literal medical model, which in turn more strongly supports the insanity defense.

> H_2: The more experience that one has had with being an expert witness concerning the issue of insanity, the more favorable one will be toward the insanity defense.

Hypothesis 2 could be explained by a number of factors: self-selection of witnesses, reinforcement, or dissonance theory.

> H_3: There will be a curvilinear relationship between short-form LRC scores and position on the insanity defense. Specifically, subjects just left of center (scores of 20 or 21) will be most favorable, subjects in the center area (17 to 19) will be moderately favorable, and subjects to either extreme (below 17 or above 21) will be least favorable.

For all three hypotheses the dependent variable is subject's position as measured by the previously described 11-point graphic scale. The six specific attitude questions on insanity will also be looked at insofar as they further clarify positions.

Hypotheses 2 and 3 will be tested for the total sample, and separately for the psychologist and psychiatrist subsamples.

RESULTS: STUDY 1

H_1: Professional Identity and Insanity Defense

As can be seen from Table 3.1, H_1 received strong support, with psychiatrists averaging 6.92 and psychologists 4.44 on the 11-point graphic scale. Even for the psychiatrists this is not a ringing endorsement of the insanity defense, with 30.9 percent placing themselves below the neutral point on the scale (6.0), and "only" 58.2 percent placing themselves on the favorable, or "valid," side of the scale. But, in contrast, 66.7 percent of the psychologists were below the neutral point and only 26.3 percent above it.

On all six attitude items the psychiatrists were more favorable toward the insanity defense. On item 9, however, the difference was negligi-

TABLE 3.1   Mean Attitude Scores Toward the Insanity Defense: Psychiatrists Versus Psychologists

Item	Psychiatrists (N = 55)	Psychologists (N = 57)	r_{pb}	p
Graphic Scale:	6.92	4.44	.357	.001
(1) The insanity defense works reasonably well for our system of justice.	2.76	2.05	.299	.001
(3) The insanity defense should be totally abolished.	2.15	2.70	.196	.02
(5) Psychiatrists, psychologists, and other mental health professionals who testify in court on insanity issues give highly unreliable testimony.	2.53	3.07	.218	.01
(7) One good argument for abolishing the insanity defense is that all adult humans are responsible for their behavior and should be punished for their wrongdoing.	2.33	3.04	.244	.005
(9) Many crimes are committed as a result of mental illness, even though the offender is not legally insane.	3.67	3.59	.029	n.s.
(10) It is important that we retain some sort of insanity defense in order that offenders who are convicted are those who are truly blameworthy.	3.58	3.19	.148	.07

NOTE: Except for the 11-point graphic scale, scores range from 1.0 to 5.0 with high scores indicating agreement with the item, and 3.0 representing a neutral point. All t-tests one-tailed.

ble. This item did not pertain directly to the insanity defense, but to the more general issue of whether the medical model was an appropriate way of viewing criminal behavior. Not shown in Table 3.1, 69.1 percent of the psychiatrists and 66.7 percent of the psychologists agreed that many crimes were a product of mental illness.

This same item (9) does, however, correlate with one's position on the graphic scale. This is true for the entire sample as a whole ($r = +.29$, $p < .001$, two-tailed), and for psychiatrists ($r = +.33$, $p < .01$, two-tailed) and psychologists ($r = +.26$, $p < .03$, two-tailed) considered separately. Thus although medical model thinking is a correlate of a pro-insanity defense position, it does not account for the difference between psychologists and psychiatrists on this issue.

H₂: Expert Witness
Experience and Insanity Defense

H_2 predicted that there would be a positive relationship between being an expert witness and one's position on the insanity defense. Expert witness was measured both as a dichotomous variable and on a continuous scale representing frequency.

As can be seen in Table 3.2, this hypothesis was supported for both measures of expert witness for the total sample. The size of the correlations decreases markedly, however, when the psychologist and psychiatrist subgroups are considered, reaching a traditionally acceptable level of significance only when the frequency measure is used with psychiatrists.

H₃: Ideology and
Insanity Defense

H_3 predicted a curvilinear relationship between LRC scores and attitude toward the insanity defense. This hypothesis was confirmed for the entire sample: eta = .372 (df 3/108, p < .01, one-tailed), as well as for each subsample. For psychiatrists, eta = .480 (df 3/51, p < .01, one-tailed), and for psychologists, eta = .376 (df 3/53, p < .01, one-tailed). As can be seen from Figure 3.1, in each case the trend of the data fits the hypothesis fairly closely. The only exception was that for psychologists, the middle-of-the-road, or center group was slightly more pro-insanity defense than was the center-left, or medical

TABLE 3.2   Correlation Between Experience as an Expert Witness and Attitude Toward the Insanity Defense

Witness Measure	Total Sample (N = 112)		Psychiatrists (N = 55)		Psychologists (N = 57)	
	r	p	r	p	r	p
Dichotomous	+.268	.002	+.224	.055	.121	.185
Total frequency	+.321	.001	+.253	.035	.182	.092

NOTE: A positive correlation indicates that those with (more) expert witness experience were more favorable toward the insanity defense.
All t-tests one-tailed.

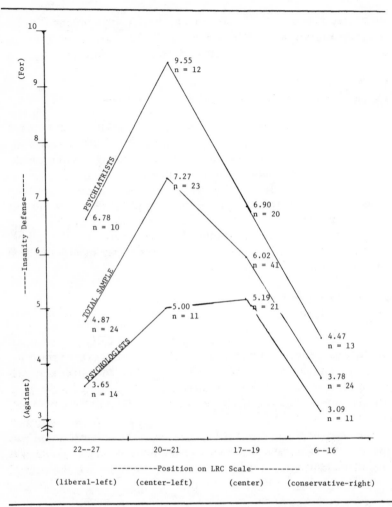

Figure 3.1 **Mean Insanity Defense Scores as a Function of LRC Position, by Profession**

model group. In each case, as predicted, the extreme left and extreme right LRC groups were more opposed to the insanity defense.

It should be noted that a significant eta in no way rules out the possibility of a linear relationship. However, the strictly linear (Pearson) correlation between LRC scores and insanity defense scores proved to be very low: r = +.059 (n.s.). This confirms the fact that, as predicted, the relationship is curvilinear.

Extraneous Variables

We indicated above that psychiatrists and psychologists differed on a number of demographic variables. The only variable with a significant relationship to insanity defense, however, proved to be age: older subjects were more supportive of the insanity defense (r = +.29, p < .002, two-tailed). Partial correlation indicated that this variable did not account for any of the other observed relationships.

Summary of Relationships

In summary, then, Study 1 found that attitude toward the insanity defense correlated with four variables: LRC, profession, expert witness experience, and age. "Acceptance of medical model thinking" (item 9, Table 3.1) might also be considered a fifth correlate, or it might be considered a component of the attitude itself (albeit a component on which psychologists and psychiatrists failed to differ). These findings provide good support for the general theory behind this research—namely, that positions on the insanity defense reflect underlying predispositions.

We have already outlined the rationale for the association between LRC scores and the insanity defense. Briefly put, both the conservative (below 17) and the very liberal (above 22) doubt the validity of the insanity defense; conservatives because they see too many escaping responsibility and punishment, liberals because they object to various aspects of the labeling process. Having established that attitudes toward the insanity defense are strongly associated with a professional's value system, it remains to be seen how this bias might affect an expert's views in a particular case. This issue is the focus of Study 2.

STUDY 2: ATTITUDE TOWARD INSANITY DEFENSE AND JUDGMENT OF INSANITY

The Case: Albert

Construction of a case to be used in this study was essentially an art. The goal was to construct a case that was realistic, that could be

This is a purely hypothetical case. You may assume that all of the following are uncontested facts.

Albert is a 49 year-old white male (d.o.b. 6-10-34). He has one sibling, a 40 year-old half-brother. He grew up in Tennessee, in a Baptist family that moved to Detroit in 1947. Both of his natural parents have been dead for over 5 years. His stepmother is still living.

Albert has no prior criminal record (except for a few speeding tickets in his twenties and a series of still unpaid and fogotten-about-by-all parking tickets over 10 years old).

He joined the Navy in 1953, but did not see any action in Korea (or elsewhere). He stayed in the Navy until 1965. He never attained any rank, but was honorably discharged.

Albert married in 1968, at age 34. His wife was a 30 year-old divorcee with two small children, then aged 2 and 4. Albert has not had any children of his own. The oldest son is no longer living at home.

(1) On January 10, 1983 Albert's wife and son leave him and move to another city (where her family lives). They have moved out once before, but reconciled. On January 25 Albert is told that his wife is filing for divorce.

(2) On February 10 Albert's foreman verbally reprimands him for sloppy, careless work. He has worked for a small tool-and-die shop for about 5 years. Albert complains that his co-workers are messing up his work area and distracting him with their dirty stories.

(3) Over the next three weeks there is an incident at work about every other day. On several occasions Albert initiates the interaction with the foreman by going to him and complaining about some of his co-workers. There are ten other employees in Albert's area of the shop. At one time or another he complains that all ten are hassling him.

(4) On March 3 the foreman orders Albert to take three days off. Albert screams at the foreman, "You can't do this to me. You won't get away with it. The Lord knows what is in your heart!" Albert smashes the timeclock with a hammer and leaves abruptly.

(5) After leaving work Albert spends several hours just driving around. (This cannot be directly verified, but there are no allegations by either prosecution or defense of any drinking.) Early that evening he stops at a local K-Mart and buys some ammunition for a 22-caliber pistol. The clerk remembers him as very quiet and soft spoken. The pistol is one that Albert purchased "for protection" in 1967. He claims that he has only used it for occasional target practice since then, perhaps about once every two or three months.

(6) At about 10:00 a.m. on March 4 Albert appears at his workplace, pulls the pistol from his lunchbucket, and shoots and kills the foreman. Then he yells at two of his co-workers, "I warned you, you filthy foul-mouthed wretches to leave me alone; now the day of wrath is at hand. God is not mocked." Albert proceeds to fire several shots at the two co-workers, killing one and seriously wounding the other. Then he turns the gun on himself and pulls the trigger, but the gun is empty. He drops the gun and walks calmly out of the shop. He offers no resistance when the police pick him up walking along the street about 10 minutes later.

(7) One week later Albert is observed to be withdrawn, subdued, depressed, and occasionally expressing remorse. At his arraignment he expresses the wish to plead guilty and "get it over with." Over his objections the judge appoints a lawyer for him. Also contrary to Albert's verbally expressed wishes, the lawyer intends to plead him temporarily insane.

Figure 3.2   Albert: Case Synopsis

briefly presented, and that would generate a difference of opinion. The case, which we call "Albert," is based on a fictionalized composite of three actual cases from our own clinical experience. With the help of a pilot study using criminal justice students, details were adjusted in the hope of achieving a range of professional opinions. The resulting case summary that was used for this study is shown in Figure 3.2

Subjects

Subjects for Study 2 were sampled from the same population base as for Study 1. In this case, however, we decided to begin with a somewhat smaller sample, in order to concentrate our efforts on a higher return rate. The sample for Study 2 consisted of 68 psychiatrists and 68 psychologists, randomly sampled from the Detroit-area yellow pages. Nonresponding subjects were sent two follow-up mailings. Complete returns were received from 36 psychologists and 29 psychiatrists. An additional 7 questionnaires were returned either unopened or incomplete. Other than profession and amount of expert witness experience, no demographic questions were asked in Study 2.

Questionnaire

The Albert Case Synopsis was accompanied by a one-page questionnaire. The graphic scale used in Study 1 was repeated. This scale was followed by the instruction to read the Albert Case Synopsis insert and then to answer the following eight questions, using a number from 5 (strongly agree) to 1 (strongly disagree):

(a) Albert is probably morally responsible for his behavior;
(b) Albert should be sentenced to prison for a very long time (or life);
(c) Albert's behavior indicates a high probability of mental illness;
(d) it is very likely that Albert's behavior was the direct result of a delusional belief system, that in turn reflects an underlying psychotic condition;
(e) Albert should probably not be held criminally responsible for his behavior;
(f) Albert belongs in a state hospital rather than a prison;
(g) there is a reasonable chance that Albert can be helped by psychotropic medication and/or psychotherapy, to the point that he would no longer be dangerous; and
(h) it would *not* be *unreasonable* to find that although Albert was legally

insane at the time of the killings, he is not (several months later) psychotic, nor is he a threat to society.

The scale was scored in Likert fashion, by adding the eight responses together. (The responses to the first two items, a and b, were reverse scored: 5 = 1, 4 = 2, 3 = 3, etc.) The total of the eight items will be referred to as the Albert Scale. Scores could range from 8 to 40, with high scores indicating the belief that Albert was legally insane. Although it was thought that all eight questions were relevant to attitude toward the insanity defense, question(e), concerning Albert's criminal responsibility, was the central question. This item, which sidesteps the definition of legal insanity, was intended to allow subjects to use their own criteria for insanity. Nevertheless, the fact that all subjects were currently practicing in Michigan—which roughly follows the American Law Institute's model definition of insanity— may have influenced how subjects responded to the entire Albert scale.

Hypotheses

The central hypothesis for this study was that attitude toward the insanity defense, as measured by the 11-point graphic scale, would be predictive of attitude toward Albert, as measured by the 8-item Albert Scale—especially item (e). This hypothesis is based on the rationale that those who perceive certain criminally deviant behavior to be a function of severe mental illness are more likely to have a generally positive attitude toward the insanity defense as a legal tool, and to be more likely to perceive insanity in any particular case.

Secondary hypotheses were that relatively favorable attitudes toward the insanity defense, as well as attitude toward Albert, would correlate with being a psychiatrist rather than a psychologist, and with amount of expert witness experience.

RESULTS: STUDY 2

The Albert Scale

The Albert Case Synopsis was intended to be a borderline case, on which one could reasonably take either a pro- or anti-insanity defense position. It is encouraging, then, that the average score on the total Albert Scale was 25.98, which is quite close to the theoretical neutral point of 24 (the score one would get by responding "don't know" to each item). On the specific question concerning Albert's legal responsibility, item (e), 32 (49 percent) respondents believed Albert should be held responsible, 21 (32 percent) believed he was not responsible, and 12 (18 percent) answered "don't know." In other words, just over half the sample were willing to give Albert's insanity plea serious consideration.

Attitudes Toward the
Insanity Defense

The mean score on the 11-point graphic scale was 6.87. If we consider scale positions 9-11 as pro-insanity defense, 27 subjects (42 percent) were in this group: There were 25 subjects (38 percent) fell in the middle range (position 4-8), and 13 subjects (20 percent) were against the insanity defense (position 1-3).

Approximately half of the subjects in the original sample for Study 1 were also in the original sample for Study 2. We do not know how much overlap there was between the subjects who actually responded to the two studies. In each study, however, subjects were invited to sign their names if they desired to receive feedback. This allowed us to match 24 names for each study, and thus to compute a measure of reliability for the graphic scale. Over an interval of six to eight months, the test-retest reliability was: $r = +.85$ ($p < .001$).

Prediction of the
Albert Scale Responses

The central hypothesis for this study was that attitude toward Albert (i.e., belief that Albert was not legally responsible) would be predictable from the more general attitude toward the insanity defense. As can be seen from Table 3.3, this hypothesis was strongly borne out. The Albert Scale correlated about as highly with attitude toward insanity defense (graphic scale) as their respective reliabilities would allow. Furthermore, each item in the Albert Scale had a significant positive correlation with attitude toward the insanity defense, and, as expected, the single best item (e) concerned the "bottom line" issue of Albert's legal responsibility.

In contrast, neither profession nor expert witness experience correlated significantly with the Albert Scale. With regard to profession,

TABLE 3.3   Attitudes Toward Albert as a Function of Insanity Defense, Profession, and Expert Witness Experience

Albert Scale		Graphic Scale		Profession[1]		Expert Witness[2]	
Item	Mean[3]	r	p	r	p	r	p
a[4]	3.54	+.42	.001	+.19	.06	−.03	−
b[4]	2.52	+.47	.001	+.08	.26	−.06	−
c	3.89	+.43	.001	+.11	.19	+.13	.15
d	3.58	+.25	.02	+.00	.50	+.11	.19
e	2.77	+.67	.001	+.16	.11	+.03	.42
f	3.13	+.47	.001	+.15	.12	+.02	.45
g	3.32	+.58	.001	+.18	.07	+.03	.40
h	3.20	+.36	.002	+.13	.16	+.01	.47
Total	25.98	+.68	.001 ·	+.16	.10	−.02	−

NOTE: All t-tests one-tailed; N = 65 throughout.
(1) "Profession" treated as a dummy variable; a positive correlation means that psychiatrists scored higher; (2) "Expert Witness" based on subjects' reports of the total amount or frequency of their experience in insanity defense cases; (3) for individual items, a score above 3.0 indicates a trend toward agreement; (4) these items were reverse-scored; high scores indicate disagreement.

all the items of the Albert Scale were in the predicted direction (psychiatrists being more likely to answer the items in a pro-insanity manner), but the differences were trivial and approached significance on only two items—(a) and (g). With regard to the amount of expert witness experience a subject had, the correlation with the Albert Scale was extremely small and in the opposite of the predicted direction.

Comparison to Study 1

The fact that neither profession nor expert witness experience correlated significantly with the Albert Scale raises the issue of whether their correlation with the graphic scale (general attitude toward the insanity defense) in Study 1 was replicated. In fact, profession still correlated strongly with the graphic scale: $r_{pb} = .32$ (p < .005, one-tailed), compared to .36 in Study 1. For expert witness experience, however, the correlation with the graphic scale was only + .06 (n.s.), down from + .32 in Study 1.

The findings with respect to expert witness experience, therefore, are open to question and certainly more work needs to be done on the relationship of this variable to attitude toward the insanity defense. At the very least it should be instructive to separate defense witness experience from prosecution witness experience. Differences in type of experience would no doubt be a function of selection bias, but they might also affect subsequent perceptions of the insanity defense.

Although profession showed a consistent correlation with insanity defense (graphic scale), the findings of Study 2 present something of an anomaly in that although the graphic scale correlated very highly with the Albert Scale, there is little correlation between profession and Albert Scale. This suggests that any given psychiatrist is likely to be more favorable toward the insanity defense than any given psychologist, but if the two were matched on general attitude toward the insanity defense, then the *psychologist* would be somewhat more likely to see insanity in Albert's particular case. This can be shown statistically by the fact that the partial correlation between profession and the Albert Scale is negative: $-.08$ (psychologists slightly more supportive of an insanity defense for Albert). In other words, professional identification (or training) does not seem to be a predictor of judgments of insanity apart from its contribution to attitudes toward insanity.

Analysis of Subsamples

Thus the main implication of our results to this point is that differences in opinions among professionals in an insanity defense case such as Albert's are based highly on generalized attitudes about the insanity defense itself. Although this finding is based on a representative sample of potential experts, it would be of interest to determine if it held especially for those subjects who would be *likely* to testify in a real life situation.

In order to explore this possibility we looked at two subsamples: those who indicated that there was at least a 50 percent chance that they would conduct an initial interview of Albert if asked to by the defense, and those who had actually had expert witness experience.

Most of the sample indicated an interest in interviewing Albert: N $= 52$ (80%). Within this group, the correlation between the Albert Scale and the insanity defense scale did drop somewhat, from $+.68$ down to $+.50$ ($p < .001$). But the correlation between insanity defense and item (e) (Albert's legal responsibility) actually went up slightly, from $+.67$ to $+.683$ ($p < .001$).

One might still protest that this subgroup may contain a high number of individuals unlikely to be actually called upon to testify, especially psychologists who are against the insanity defense. As one might expect, the psychologists in our sample were much less likely to have testified as expert witnesses in insanity cases (r_{pb} = .41, p < .001). Therefore, a second subgroup was looked at: those subjects who had had expert witness experience. This group had an N of 24, 18 of whom overlapped with the "willing to interview" subgroup. For this "experience" group, the correlation between the Albert and the insanity defense scale was + .55 (p < .005), down slightly from the total sample. For item (e), however, the correlation rose to an extremely high + .80 (p < .001).

Thus the subgroup analyses tend to further support our general conclusion that there is a strong relationship between a professional's attitude toward the insanity defense and his or her testimony in a particular case.

DISCUSSION

Summary

The two studies reported here have explored the links between personal-attitudinal variables, generalized attitude toward the insanity defense, and the effect of that attitude on judgment in a particular case. Study 1 found that attitude toward the insanity defense was a function of ideology (beliefs about social versus individual responsibility for crime), professional identification (psychiatry versus psychology), amount of expert witness experience, and age. Study 2 replicated the relationship between profession and insanity defense, but failed to replicate the effect of expert witness experience. (Age was not measured.) More importantly, Study 2 found that attitude toward the insanity defense in general was a powerful predictor of how subjects judged the particular case of Albert, correlating + .68 with the Albert Scale and + .67 with belief in Albert's insanity (item e). The practical significance of these correlations is shown in Table 4. Of the 27 subjects who were strongly in favor of the insanity defense, 21 (78 percent) did not feel that Albert was responsible; in contrast, of the 13 subjects who were strongly against the insanity defense, all felt that Albert was responsible.

As strong as this relationship is, it was even stronger when we looked at subjects who had previously given expert witness testimony in an insanity defense case; for these subjects, the correlation between the

TABLE 3.4   Relief in Albert's Sanity as a Function of Attitude
Toward the Insanity Defense

Attitude Toward Insanity Defense		*Is Albert Responsible*[1]		*Albert Scale*[2]	
Scale Score	*N*	*No* *N (%)*	*Yes* *N (%)*	*High* *N (%)*	*Low* *N (%)*
Pro (9-11)	27	21 (78)	6 (22)	23 (85)	4 (15)
Neutral (4-8)	25	12 (48)	13 (52)	14 (56)	11 (44)
Anti (1-3)	13	0 (0)	13 (100)	1 (8)	12 (92)

1. Based on subjects' responses to item e; a response of 1, 2, or 3 (disagree or don't know) was categorized as "no." 2. Based on the total scale, including item e; scores of 25 and above were categorized as high.

insanity defense scale and belief in Albert's lack of legal responsibility (item e) reached + .80.

The Problem of Generalization

We clearly mean to imply that this research indicates something about how psychiatrists and clinical psychologists reach their conclusions in real insanity cases. There are, however, four objections that can be raised to our making this generalization.

The most basic objection concerns whether a paper-and-pencil response to a paper-and-pencil case, perhaps involving 20 minutes of a subject's time, has much to do with how that subject would behave in a real-life case. Such paper-and-pencil measures have a long and controversial history, dating back at least to the classic LaPiere study (1934), through Carl Hovland's (1959) work on the difference between field and laboratory studies, and Campbell's (1957, 1963) concern about external validity and the need for multimethod approaches and nomothetic nets. We can only concur that paper-and-pencil research should not be seen as a substitute for field research on this issue. At the same time, however, paper-and-pencil tests add a degree of control and replicability not possible in field research. We also feel that most of the responding subjects took the questionnaire seriously. In Study 2, for example, 34 subjects (52 percent) requested feedback from the study, or wrote unsolicited explanatory comments about their responses.

The second problem with generalization concerns whether Albert is at all typical of insanity cases. That is, even if our results would generalize to a real-life Albert, would they generalize to other cases?

Perhaps Albert was a unique case that somehow "activated" general insanity defense attitudes. Of course, there is no "typical" insanity case, and there is virtually no limit on the variations one could run on Albert. Although we can see no reason why the relationship between insanity defense attitudes and particular judgments would not continue to occur, any final answer will require further research.

The third problem concerns our sample. Although Study 2 received some return from 53 percent of the original sample, and a usable return from 48 percent, it is always possible that the nonresponders were somewhat different. Furthermore, even if the nonresponders would have shown the same pattern of responses as the responders, there would still be no guarantee that this would hold for other samples of psychiatrists and clinical psychologists. Although this criticism can be made of any research, it may be especially true here because of the fourth generalization problem.

This fourth problem concerns the definition of insanity and the procedures used in implementing an insanity defense in a particular state. Definitions differ from state to state as do the judicial procedures involved. In Michigan, for example, testimony is always available from a forensic center clinician, who is "neutral" in that he is commissioned by the state rather than the defense or prosecutor. About 90 percent of the time, judges or juries agree with his or her testimony (Smith and Hall, 1982). Juries in Michigan have the option of a "guilty but mentally ill" verdict; although this has been found to have little effect on trial outcome (Smith and Hall, 1982), it may have some unknown effect on the expert witness testimony involved. Once again, we can only say that replication under other conditions is called for.

Implications for the
Insanity Defense

Assuming that the generalization problems can be surmounted, it is still problematic as to what the practical implications of our results are. On the face of it, these results certainly lend more support to the critics than to the defenders of the insanity defense. Any widespread change in the judicial system, however, must take into account much more than the credibility of expert witnesses. The insanity defense has been viewed as a kind of linchpin that holds together the broader system of responsibility-desert-punishment (Ingram, 1983; Insanity Defense Work Group, 1983; Slowinski, 1982). About fifteen years ago when the judicial system's move away from punishment had reached its peak (Kennedy and Kelly, 1981), it was possible to argue that the concept of blame might better be abandoned for all offenders (Menninger, 1966). If this were to be done, excusing someone on grounds of severe mental illness would cease to be relevant. But the current trend is certainly back toward a justice model, stressing moral and legal responsibility and deserved punishment (Fogel, 1975; Von Hirsch, 1976). Therefore, some mechanism will be needed to excuse (from punishment, if not detention) those whom society views as incapable of conforming to the law. Thus Morris (1983), who argues for the abolition of the insanity defense as such, still accomplishes the same objective by permitting the introduction of evidence—including psychiatric evidence—relevant to the mental state of the individual.

It is something of a cliche to say that ultimately the decision on insanity is in the hands of the jury. Having said it, some find this a source of optimism; others are dismayed. The most thorough investigation of juries' reactions to insanity defense testimony reached a basically optimistic conclusion—namely, that juries are capable of weighing conflicting psychiatric testimony and drawing reasonable conclusions (Simon, 1967).

We hypothesize that what is most helpful to a jury in making its decision about a defendant's legal responsibility is not the experts' bottom-line opinions as to sanity or insanity, but their (sometimes competing, sometimes complementary) explanations about the defendant's motivation. Based on this assumption, we feel that a reasonable conclusion to be reached from our data is that experts' testimony should be limited to their opinions about the defendant's mental or motivational state (at the time before and during the offense). We believe that this would help make it clear to the jury that it is the jury's role to make the value judgment as to whether that mental state was extreme enough to warrant exculpation.

One could raise the objection that by having experts testify about mental states we have only pushed the problem back one step: Won't these experts still base their opinion on their general attitudes about the insanity defense? There is some evidence that this might not happen. As an inspection of Table 3.3 illustrates, Albert Scale item (e)—concerning legal responsibility—was most susceptible to bias. In contrast, the item that correlated least with insanity defense attitudes concerned the dynamics of Albert's behavior, item (d). Furthermore, this low correlation (+ .25) did not occur simply because subjects could not agree with the capsule diagnosis of Albert that item (d) presented: 36 subjects (60 percent) agreed with item (d) and only 10 (15 percent) disagreed, with the rest indicating "don't know."

Thus attitudes toward the insanity defense account for a large part of the variance in opinions about legal responsibility (45 percent), but only a small part of the variance in opinions about underlying psychodynamics (6 percent). This difference in variance is highly significant: $t = 3.09$, df 62, $p < .01$, two-tailed.

CONCLUSION

Many value-related issues interconnect with the insanity defense. In this research we have traced the antecedents and consequences of belief in the validity and usefulness of that defense. We have concluded that leaving the judgment about legal insanity strictly to the judge or jury reinforces the idea that beliefs about the locus of criminal responsibility are essentially a matter of applying one's personal ideology to observable data, rather than a function of objective, scientific expertise.

REFERENCES

CAMPBELL, D. T. (1957) "Factors relevant to the validity of experiments in social settings." Psychological Bulletin, 54: 297-312.

———(1963) "Social attitudes and other acquired behavioral dispositions," pp. 94-176 in S. Koch (ed.), Psychology: A Study of a Science. Vol. 6, Investigations of Man as Socius. New York: McGraw-Hill.

CHRISTENSON, R. (1983) "From Hadfield to Hinckley: the insanity plea in politically related trials." Presented at the Academy of Criminal Justice Sciences meeting, San Antonio, Texas.

CLARKE, J. W. (1982) American Assasins. Princeton, NJ: Princeton University Press.

FOGEL, D. (1975) We Are the Living Proof: The Justice Model for Corrections. Cincinnati: Anderson.

HOVLAND, C. I. (1959) "Reconciling conflicting results derived from experimental and survey studies of attitude change." American Psychologist 14: 8-17.

INGRAM, J. (1983) "Changing the insanity defense: the assault on the *mens rea* conception of crime," Presented at the Academy of Criminal Justice Sciences meeting, San Antonio, Texas.

Insanity Defense Work Group (1983) American Psychiatric Association Statement on the Insanity Defense. American Journal of Psychiatry, 140: 681-688.

KENNEDY, D. B. and T. M. KELLY (1981) "The swinging pendulum of correctional reform." Criminal Justice Review 6: 44-47.

LaPIERE, R. T. (1934) "Attitudes vs. actions." Social Forces 13: 230-237.

LILLYQUIST, M. J. (1980) Understanding and Changing Criminal Behavior. Englewood Cliffs, NJ: Prentice-Hall.

LOCKWOOD, R. W. (1983) "The insanity defense; reactions and reforms." Presented at the Academy of Criminal Justice Sciences meeting, San Antonio, Texas.

MacNAMARA, D. (1977) "The medical model in corrections." Criminology, 14: 137-152.

MENNINGER, K. (1966) The Crime of Punishment. New York: Viking.

MILLER, W. B. (1973) "Ideology and criminal justice policy: some current issues." Journal of Criminal Law and Criminology 64: 141-162.

MONAHAN, J. (1973) "Abolish the insanity defense? Not yet." Rutgers Law Review 26: 719-740.

MORRIS, M. (1976) Instead of Prisons: A Handbook for Abolitionists. Syracuse, NY: Prison Research Action Project.

MORRIS N. (1982) Madness and the Criminal Law. Chicago: University of Chicago Press.

SHAH, S. A. (1974) "Some interactions of law and mental health in the handling of social deviance." Catholic University Law Review 23: 674-719.

SIMON R. J. (1967) The Jury and the Defense of Insanity. Boston: Little, Brown.

SLOWINSKI, K. (1982) "Criminal responsibility: changes in the insanity defense and the "guilty but mentally ill" response." Washburn Law Journal 21: 515-554.

SMITH, G. and J. HALL (1982) "Evaluating Michigan's guilty but mentally ill verdict: an empirical study." Journal of Law Reform 16: 77-114.

STOLL, C. S. (1968) Images of man and social control. Social Forces 47: 119-127.

SZASZ, T. S. (1960) "The myth of mental illness." American Psychologist 15: 113-118.

———(1968) Law, Liberty and Psychiatry. New York: Collier.

VON HIRSCH, A. (1976) Doing Justice. New York: Hill and Wang.

4.

SOCIAL SCIENTISTS IN THE COURTROOM:
The Frustrations of
Two Expert Witnesses

Marc G. Gertz
Edmond J. True
Florida State University

The purpose of the following presentation is to explore reasons for the tension between social science and the law. Our academic interest in this topic arose from our practical experience as expert witnesses in a murder trial in Penascola, Florida. The case involved the prosecution of a woman who killed her husband by shooting him at least seven times with five different guns while he slept. At her trial the defendent claimed self-defense. The case attracted a great deal of media attention due to the somewhat unusual theory of the defense: The defendant relied on the testimony of an expert witness, a feminist psychologist, who claimed, based on her research, that this murder was inevitable because the wife suffered from the battered wife syndrome and learned helplessness. According to their expert, these two concepts could be used to describe a pattern in which severe abuse (both physical and psychological) evolves into a form of psychological paralysis for the victim (the wife), who cannot bring herself to leave the damaging and dangerous environment.

We entered this case when the prosecutor requested us to evaluate the defense expert's testimony and the credibility of the research upon which the testimony was based. A cursory reading of the expert's research indicated a litany of errors that any properly trained social scientist would have discovered. However, lawyers are not social scientists, and just communicating our conclusions to the prosecutor took many months. First, we had to train the prosecutor in the rudiments of social science research. He was very willing to learn, and after a series of sessions with him we felt that he understood the topics we wished to discuss.

Yet as our role expanded, the initial frustration of trying to educate the prosecuting attorney on proper methodology and points of attack seemed slight by comparison when it came time to interact with the judge and defense counsel. For example, in responding to vigorous cross-examination by the defense attorney it became necessary for us to stop the line of questioning and correct the attorney's use of the term "dependent variable." He clearly meant independent variable, and to have answered his question as asked would have misled everyone involved. If such elementary concepts as dependent and independent variables raise problems, how does one go about trying to explain stepwise multiple regression?

At this point we seriously began to question what we were doing in a courtroom. Our original role had grown from trying to educate the prosecutor about social science methods to testifying in a murder trial. The more we testified, and the longer the defense cross-examined us, the more it became obvious that we were not communicating. It was not that these attorneys lacked intelligence—quite the opposite appeared to be the case. The communication failure occurred because we spoke such dramatically different languages and used such widely disparate paradigms. What became obvious to us was this: Lawyers do not comprehend what social scientists know, and social scientists do not present information in a manner that is particularly useful in a courtroom setting.

This experience could lead to the conclusion that the major source of the problem is simply a failure to communicate. The following presentation will suggest that the difficulty is more deeply rooted than that. It inheres in the differences between the nature and purpose of law and the social sciences.

A portion of the controversy over social science knowledge in the courtroom can be traced to the role of political ideology in shaping views of law and social science. It can be suggested that the purpose of law is political end and that policy choices—or even choices about evidence—are determined by political considerations. A similar argument frequently is leveled against the kinds of research conducted by social science and the resultant conclusions.

This presentation sees a broad definition of ideology, one that includes views on the nature of law and social science, as a more fundamental concern. One of the central distinctions between the nature of law and social science is the proper mechanism for pursuing truth. The ideology of the law suggests that an adversary system is the best way of finding truth. Social science requires a presentation of all the evidence, supportive and contradictory, and a process of replication prior to accepting a generalization as part of knowledge. The tension between the adversary and scientific approaches to knowledge creates a situation in which social science evidence complicates the trial process.

In an attempt to clarify the dimensions associated with making a choice about the usefulness of social science in the courtroom, an individual's position can be broken down into two issues. The first deals with a factual question—Is the material, as presented, evidence that will be accepted in a courtroom given the current tests used by the legal profession? For the social scientist the critical factual issue focuses on whether the body of knowledge lives up to current standards of inquiry. With respect to appellate decisions, it is difficult to identify what specific tests are being applied to make the determination about the evidentiary value of social science. Given the earlier discussion it appears to be an assessment as to whether the material fits into the dimensions of the legal question. At the trial level, however, the specifics of the tests are spelled out in the law. Expert testimony must (1) be relevant to the issue at hand; (2) meet the three qualifications that traditionally govern the admissibility of expert testimony—the subject matter must be beyond the ken of the average layman, the expert must have sufficient knowledge in the area, and the evidence must be supported by sufficient knowledge in the field—and (3) have probative value that outweighs its potential prejudicial impact (McCormick, 1972). Although this series of tests seems to place the factual choice into a narrow range, that is not necessarily true. It has been argued, for example, that the more detailed the rules, the more discretion there is involved in making choices (Pepinsky, 1976).

The second issue deals with a normative question: Regardless of the immediate merits of the material, should it or could it be used as evidence of fact? Our argument is that, in a central tendency sense, members of the two communities approach this decision with different points of reference for answering the question. The narrow conception of ideology as politics clearly plays a role here. In addition, the legal profession's view of the substance and process of the law (legal ideology) influences this choice (McCleary, et al., 1981).

The answer to these two questions creates a fourfold method for examining the positions on social science as evidence. The problem is that because the legal profession has different factual and normative points of reference from the social science community, two typologies are envisioned. Figure 4.1 presents the typologies for law and social science.

Social science absolutists argue that this type of evidence is necessary to make rational choices. It has been suggested that the justices use

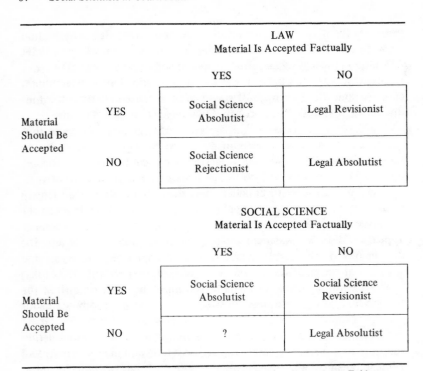

Figure 4.1   Lawyers and Social Scientists on Social Science Expertise as Evidence of Legal Fact

intuitive probablistic reasoning and that scientific calculations are simply more precise (Finklestein, 1966). On the normative side, it is suggested that expertise is used to pursue a collective good and that statistics will, in the long run, flush out discriminatory practices (DeCani, 1974).

Legal absolutists, on the other hand, argue that social science is too tentative in its ability to make definitive statements (Cahn, 1955). The normative proscription derived from the factual choice also shares a common logic; law organizes the fundamental aspects of human relationships and, as such, it cannot be based upon predictive probablistic estimates of human activity (Moynihan, 1979).

The absolutists' debate is supportive of the premise that the argument over social science as evidence is largely based in political ideology. It is the other components of the typologies that expand the scope of the argument. Social science rejectionists are concerned that the introduction of science into decision making violates the normative tenets of our jurisprudence. An example would be the concern over the use of testimony on the dangerousness of the individual and the determination of sentencing in capital cases (Cahn, 1955; Moynihan, 1979). Lacking due process and the power of an adversary proceeding, the individual is subjected to the danger of scientific sentencing outside of the traditional legal model. Unfortunately, there does not appear to be a social science counterpart to this position.

The revisionist position in both law and social science argues that social science evidence is not widely accepted as a form of evidence, but that it should be. The justification for these positions, however, demonstrates a dramatic divergence of views. A comparison of two revisionist positions indicates that the final choice hinges upon a different view of the world. Toch (1982), for example, relies heavily upon the scientific community to eventually resolve the problems of evidence and virtually ignores the role of law as a check. Thar (1982), on the other hand, assumes the facts to be properly supported and insists that the law can check excesses. Finally, it should be noted that Dix (1981) and Thar are not that far apart; Dix simply cannot find any of the legal correctives that become central to the normative choice in his area of concern.

The final component of this presentation develops, in more detail, the observed differences between social scientists (such as Toch) and lawyers (such as Thar) on this perplexing diagonal of the typologies. The specific example of the battered wife syndrome will serve as the vehicle for this analysis.

THE SPECIFIC DIMENSIONS
OF THE PROBLEM

The current status of the battered wife syndrome as evidence in criminal trials is problematic. Some jurisdictions have accepted this type of evidence by examining the rules of evidence and the specifics of the individual situation (Robinson, 1981). Others have excluded this type of testimony because it does not meet the relevance test; this applies in general, or may only apply to the specific case in question. In none of these situations is the scientific acceptability of the evidence an issue.

The cyclical nature of the battered wife syndrome is essential to many of the situations in which this type of evidence is going to be used in a self-defense argument. In order to successfully use self-defense in this situation it is necessary to show that the amount of force used was reasonable and prudent. It must also be demonstrated that the defendant, in a perceptual sense, is in immediate danger (Thar, 1982). The three stages of the syndrome—minor abuse and tension building; brutal violence, and loving period—are essential. Take the case of *State v. Curry,* for example (Eber, 1981). Mrs. Curry shot her husband while sitting in a car when no physical abuse was taking place at all. However, the battered wife syndrome suggests that the abused party becomes aware of cues to the impending onset of the brutal violence stage. Perceptually, this places the abused party in immediate danger. The defendant's past experiences with the level of physical violence can also allow her to assess the amount of force that is going to be necessary to thwart the impending attack. In a sense, it is only the defendant who can make assessments about immediacy and amount of force because only she has the experiential frame of reference.

The legal community, lacking any countervailing argument, appears to be willing to accept the origins of the battered wife syndrome as residing in the accepted methodology of the social sciences. The Court of Appeals for the District of Columbia has held, in *Ibn-Thomas v. United States* (1979), that the knowledge presented by a defense witness met the criteria of scientific knowledge (407 A2nd 626: 1376-38). The prosecution, in this instance, simply relied upon the novel scientific techniques test and did not proffer any testimony attacking the research behind the theory. Likewise, journal articles arguing for expansion of the use of this type of evidence apply unusual tests of expertise and accepted scientific knowledge. One such presentation suggests that a Dr. Vicki Boyd had done extensive research on the subject of the battered wife syndrome, yet an examination of the various reference guides to the social sciences reveals no citations for a Vicki Boyd.

The dynamics of the argument over accepting the battered wife syndrome as evidence change substantially when a counterargument on the scientific nature of the evidence is presented. Lenore Walker, one of the primary spokespersons for the battered wife syndrome in both the scientific and legal communities, was offered as an expert witness in *Hawthorne v. State* (1982). In the second trial of Ms. Jennings/Hawthorne the trial court judge excluded the testimony of Dr. Walker without hearing testimony relating to the expert/expertise criteria. The decision of the trial court judge was reversed on appeal and the prosecution decided to attack the scientific basis of the battered wife syndrome for the impending third trial. It was at this juncture that we entered into the world of law and expertise on behalf of the prosecution.

The specific points of attack on the theory of learned helplessness and the battered wife syndrome were developed from an examination of a study directed by Dr. Walker under the aegis of NIMH (Walker, 1978). The distillation of this refutation can be summarized in four points: (1) the levels of generalization presented in relationship to the data collected; (2) the operationalization, or lack thereof, of concepts central to the analysis; (3) the reliability and validity of the measures employed; and (4) the stated ideological bias of the research methodology. It was the presentation of these arguments and the resultant counterattacks that created the problems at the trial.

Initially, there is a serious problem in communication involved in this type of interchange. For example, it is not self-evident that a lawyer, during the process of cross-examination, can recognize the proper point of attack in a methodological discussion. A central issue emerged in the Hawthorne case was the problem associated with an overtly ideological piece of research. Trying to explain the role of ideology in research under direct examination is difficult enough; a proper cross-examination could punch several holes in this argument. It was our experience, however, that even when the defense attorney stumbled into the area of value neutrality and objectivity, he could not bring one of the most perplexing problems in the philosophy of the social sciences into a proper perspective for the case at hand and quickly abandoned questioning in the area.

The problem of communication also plays a role in the nature of testimony given by the social scientist. After our initial dealings with the prosecuting attorney we decided not to use several telling points of attack because of the sophistication needed to understand the methodology employed. In particular, to discuss the improper use of regression analysis while we were struggling to get the legal community to understand reliability seemed a waste of time.

The exchange over the appropriateness of Walker's methodology took place within the context of an adversary proceedings that Dix (1981) and Thar (1982) emphasize as critical to resolving issues at law. But how do you resolve the swearing contest that necessarily develops when experts testify for both parties in a dispute? The law, at least in some instances, has an answer. For example, a trial court judge's exclusion of an expert witness because in the past the expert appeared more as an advocate (ideologue) than as a witness was overturned on appeal because "it is exclusive province of the jury, not the trial court, to pass upon the credibility of a witness . . ." and this type of factor merely goes to the weight given to the testimony and not to its admissibility (More v. Huntington National Bank, 1977: 590).

Again, the ambiguity exists. An expert is admitted to testify because the knowledge transmitted is beyond the ken of the average layman, yet the jury is charged with assessing competing arguments about social science methodology. Thus the adversary process is joined with the ingrained idea that a jury is the final resolver of fact—res adjudicata— and the strength of the ideological commitment to the law is further enhanced.

For social science there is a far more serious consequence in relying upon traditional legal remedies for determining the acceptability of expertise. Consider the legal history surrounding the use of the battered wife syndrome as evidence in criminal trials.

The case of *Berle v. State* (1981) demonstrates the initial difficulty that advocacy creates for social science. In this specific instance, the testimony of Dr. Walker was ruled to be irrelevant by the Supreme Court of Wyoming. More importantly, the appellate court held that the expert could not find facts in the Berle situation that corresponded to her own cyclical theory of abuse. If the developer of the theory cannot apply the generalities to a specific case, how can a jury—even with the process of cross examination—assess the weight of the testimony?

The social scientist as advocate is further amplified by the case at hand—*Hawthorne v. State* (1982). The inclusion of physical violence within the development of the battered syndrome is widely documented (Schneider and Jordan, 1978). Yet in the Hawthorne situation there is unanimous agreement that no physical violence was present for a five-year period prior to the homicide. The only overt act by the victim directed against the defendant was on the night of the shooting when he threw a hamburger at her. As an advocate, Dr. Walker was quite willing to extend the logic of physical abuse and its role in the three stages of the syndrome to include psychological abuse. A social scientist might hypothesize that physical and psychological abuse have the same consequences and then proceed to collect data for testing, but would not state that the hypothesis was fact.

The consequences of Berle and Hawthorne are far-reaching. An individual who has strived so hard to be recognized as a social scientist, in a methodological sense, is placed into situations in which he or she cannot apply pertinent theories or when he or she has to extend ideas beyond the recognizable scope of the data that is available.

But this is not the end of the role of advocacy in the Hawthorne case. After the prosecution introduced the witnesses attacking the methodology of Walker's research the defense introduced another expert witness to support the credentials of Dr. Walker and her work. Dr. Richard Gelles, a recognized scholar in the area of family violence, was brought in to testify.

Gelles's initial position on the research conducted by Walker was that, given the state of the art, she was as good as there was and that it was much easier to destroy than to build theories. A problem with this position is that Gelles earlier raised many of the same methodological criticisms as the prosecution witnesses for the entire field of research into family violence (Gelles, 1982). In addition, he specifically leveled methodological criticisms against Dr. Walker (Gelles, 1982). Under cross-examination on these apparent inconsistencies, Gelles responded that he no longer accepted the arguments in his published work.

Once again advocacy played havoc with the traditional mechanisms of scientific inquiry for checking erroneous arguments. An article published in 1982 and written in 1981 that no longer reflects the author's view in July of 1982 does not bode well for the already shaky image of social science held by the legal profession. If advocacy for ideology can lead an individual away from the basic tenets of applying theory to fact, then advocacy for other motivations can lead to ambiguities about what the criteria for a science are.

CONCLUSIONS

The general dimensions of the problems associated with the acceptance of social science expertise as evidence in legal proceedings demonstrate that some of the disagreement is traceable to ideological positions. For some in the legal profession the critical question is not the use of the evidence but that this evidence must be presented within the established structure of the law. This reliance upon the ideals of due process and adversary proceedings is reflective of a broader definition of ideology that also encompasses law-related values.

The discussion of the acceptability of the battered wife syndrome as evidence in a criminal trial highlights both the difficulties associated with communicating knowledge across disciplines and the problems created by the social scientist as advocate. It is this last point that proves most troublesome for the role of social science in the courtroom.

Marvin Wolfgang (1974) has clearly outlined the dimensions of the problems caused by advocacy. Wolfgang, however, is willing to accept the price associated with selectively choosing only the positive (at the exclusion of the negative) because this is what the law is all about. Alice Rivlin (1973) has gone even further, suggesting the development of a "forensic social science" in which the expert brings all of his or her skills to the support of advocacy and develops a position simply to support one side of a legal argument. We feel that our examples clearly demonstrate the consequences of this view of the role of social science.

Kalmuss et al. (1982) have explored empirically the political conflicts associated with expert testimony. The tensions that are inherent in supporting a position distinct from ideology or discipline can cause individual problems. To date, no one has discussed the consequences to social science inquiry of adopting an entirely new set of rules for determining what constitutes the truth.

It may seem from our presentation that we feel the problems between the social scientists and the legal community are intractable. This is not true. We do feel that overcoming the inherent differences between the approaches of the two groups will be difficult. But, before we would say that social scientists should refrain from entering the courtroom as experts, examinations of remedies should be pursued. For example, we would like to see whether it would not be possible to have the social scientist work for the court—not the prosecution or the defense, but the court. The role of the adversaries would be to attack the expert, but the role of the expert would be more clearly defined in a neutral manner. How the judge would extract the relevant information from the expert would be a problem given our present approach to the introduction of evidence, but this is a problem in which the social scientist and the lawyer can work together. Social science has a value for the legal profession. What must be explored is how the social scientist's approach and the needs of lawyers can be integrated.

CASES

BERLE v. STATE (1981) 627 P. 2nd 1374
HAWTHORNE v. STATE (1982) 408 So. 2nd 801
IBN-THOMAS v. UNITED STATES (1979) 407 A 2nd 626
MORE v. HUNTINGTON NATIONAL BANK OF COLUMBUS (1977) 352 So. 2nd 589 NOTES
STATE v. GALLOWAY (1979) 275 N.W. 2nd 736

REFERENCES

CAHN, E. (1955 "Jurisprudence." New York University Law Review 30: 630.
DeCANI, J. (1974) "Statistical evidence in jury discrimination cases." Journal of Criminal Law and Criminology 65: 238.
DIX, G. (1981) "Expert prediction testimony in capital sentencing." American Criminal Law 19: 1.

EBER, L. (1981) "The battered wife's dilemma: to kill or be killed." Hastings Law Journal 32: 895.

FINKLESTEIN, M. (1966) "The application of statistical decision theory to the jury discrimination cases." Harvard Law Review 80: 338.

GELLES, R. (1982) "Applying research on family violence to clinical practice." Journal of Marriage and the Family 44: 9.

KALMUSS, CHESLER, and SANDERS (1982) "Political conflict and applied scholarship: expert witnesses in school desegregation litigation." Social Problems 30: 168.

McCLEARY, R., M.J. O'NEILL, T. EPPERLEIN, C. JONES, and R. H. GRAY (1981) "Effects of legal education and work experiences on perceptions of crime seriousness." Social Problems 28: 276.

McCORMICK, C. (1972) Handbook of the Law of Evidence. St. Paul, MN: West.

MOYNIHAN, D. (1979) "Social science and the courts." Public Interest 54 (Winter): 12.

PEPINSKY, H. (1976) Crime and Conflict. New York: Academic.

RIVLIN, A. (1973) "Forensic social science." Harvard Educational Review 43: 61.

ROBINSON, J. (1981) "Defense strategies for battered women who assault their mates: State v. Curry." Harvard Women's Law Journal 4: 61.

SCHNEIDER, E. and S. JORDAN (1978) "Representation of women who defend themselves in response to physical or sexual assault." Journal of Criminal Defense 4: 141.

THAR, A. (1982) "The admissibility of expert testimony on battered wife syndrome." Northwestern University Law Review 88: 348.

TOCH, H. (1982) "The role of the expert on prison conditions: the battle of footnotes in Rhodes v. Chapman." Criminal Law Bulletin 18: 38.

WALKER, L. (1978) Final Report: The Battered Women Syndrome Study (NIMH grant R01MH30147).

WOLFGANG, M. (1974) "The social scientist in court." Journal of Criminal Law and Criminology 65: 239.

III.

Comparison of Different Types of Criminal Courts

Many of the available studies of criminal courts are case-specific. When intrigued with a pattern of decision making or when testing particular hypotheses about judicial behavior, social scientists frequently look at single jurisdictions. In the most pristine form of case study, researchers focus on a single court, describe its processes, and proffer some explanation for observed behavior. When testing specific hypotheses about court processes or decision outcomes, researchers advance particular propositions and analyze the data in an effort to support or refute the proposed relationships. In many of these studies the data are culled from single jurisdictions, frequently within a limited period of time. Although case studies and single jurisdiction analyses are valuable methods in their own right, there is a need for comparative scrutiny if we are going to be able to generalize to groups or systems of courts. Comparative inquiry by definition focuses on more than one jurisdiction. The researcher can study two or more jurisdictions in a more general system (e.g., comparing superior courts in Atlanta and Macon within the state of Georgia); courts in two or more general systems (e.g., courts in Atlanta, Georgia and Tallahassee, Florida); two or more general systems (e.g., felony courts in Georgia and Florida); or even two or more types of legal systems (e.g., juvenile versus adult).

Not surprisingly, there are not many comparative analyses of criminal court behavior and decisions. It is difficult and costly to obtain the data and it is burdensome to control for jurisdictional variations that may impact decision processes. Suppose, for example, you were interested in studying sentencing disparities in Georgia and New York. Because offense severity is a critical variable, you would have to control for its effect. However, the criminal code of Georgia may not classify or define an offense in the same manner as New York. This makes it difficult to compare the sentences administered for offenders who may actually commit the same crime or engage in similar behavior.

The two chapters in this section draw the reader's attention to comparative inquiry. In the first selection Gary Keveles compares the military court system to civilian adult and juvenile structures. Focusing on court processing, he looks at underlying philosophical approaches, organizational structures, and role specifications. Concluding that military justice offers attributes unique to that system, he proffers a reform strategy that requires a broader comparative focus—namely cross-national.

The second chapter consists of a review of the literature on state and federal courts processes in a specific area of criminal law. Looking at the allegations of federal court superiority (specifically, the claim that defendants' rights are more strongly supported in federal courts than state forums), Call searched for all evidence that was drawn from comparative studies. Reviewing these studies, he concludes that federal courts are somewhat more liberal than state courts. He cautions against any exaggeration of the difference, however, as the evidence is not as great as more traditional expectations would have us believe.

The Keveles and Call chapters feature comparative analyses of types of legal systems and demonstrate the need for more social science investigations of that genre if we are going to be able to speak confidently of courts as systems.

5.

THE THIRD SYSTEM OF JUSTICE:
Military Justice

Gary N. Keveles
University of Missouri—St. Louis

Three systems of justice coexist in the United States: criminal, juvenile, and military. These social control systems are different in philosophical orientation, objectives, procedures, and type of persons regulated. Yet in many respects they closely parallel each other. Each is a societal instrument established to prevent and control deviant behavior among a class of individuals. All are organized to formally test alleged violations by invoking involuntary court proceedings. They also share an authority to deprive a person of his or her liberty, a most severe form of permissible state intrusion. They all have the capability of tagging a person with a stigmatizing label such as criminal, delinquent, or dishonorable.

Curiously, we know much about criminal and juvenile justice but little about military justice. Perhaps only during times of armed conflict or national crisis does our attention turn to this third leg of the American justice tripod. Yet over two million people are actively serving in our peacetime armed forces today (Department of Defense, 1983). This number is larger than the populations of sixteen of our states (Bureau of the Census, 1983). Most members of the service are males 18-24 years old, demographics often associated with the civilian crime problem. Comparison of these military demographics to similar state populations would reveal, however, that the scope of military power is much greater than that of sixteen states. For example, 43 states have fewer 18-24-year-olds than the military has (Bureau of the Census, 1980; Department of Defense, 1981).

Author's Note: *This research was supported in part by the Center for International Studies and by a research fellowship from the Office of Research Administration, University of Missouri—St. Louis.*

The military justice system's reputation is not good. Problems with the way it has operated have provoked, after every major war, intense outcrys to drastically reform it (Sherman, 1970). One frequently hears that "military justice is to justice as military music is to music." One knows that servicemembers are not entitled to exercise the same civil liberties they have sworn to defend with their lives—a sad paradox, to say the least. Despite these criticisms and shortcomings, however, military justice has been in the forefront of many legal changes. Examples of three procedural developments are as follows: (1) warning of rights, (2) plea bargaining, and (3) discovery. In *Miranda v. Arizona* (1966) the U.S. Supreme Court made reference to the rights warnings given servicemembers for 18 years in justifying the feasibility of applying such warnings to civilians prior to custodial interrogation. Military plea bargaining was recognized and regulated twenty years before the U.S. Supreme Court did the same in *Santobello v. New York* in 1971. Pretrial argreements are reduced to writing, containing all the terms to which the parties have agreed, and have been closely monitored by military appellate courts. Servicemembers have a greater certainty than civilian defendants that their bargain will be kept. Pretrial discovery rights, a practical advantage for the accused in preparing for trial and affecting the trial's outcome, is far more liberal in the military than in federal and state jurisdictions (Kadish et al., 1982). Discovery rights of servicemembers are almost without restriction (Moyer, 1970). In some ways, then, military justice has adopted procedures that have been or could be beneficial to civilian court defendants. This all suggests that what we know about military justice is not proportionate to its significance in regulating the lives of Americans, and that this system could serve in some ways as a model to emulate.

This chapter brings attention to military justice—a rich, unexplored research arena—by comparing its middle stages of processing, which are court-dominated, with similar stages in criminal and juvenile justice. Both criminal and juvenile court processes offer useful reference points in helping to understand military courts. They are courts that operate at different starting points from each other and move toward different goals. The criminal and juvenile justice features portrayed here, however, are not total reflections of these systems. These are complex justice systems with divergent, and even, contradictory ideologies and practices. Rather, sections of these systems are outlined and then compared to the military justice context, clarifying attributes of military justice. This analysis will show that some elements of military justice resemble criminal justice components; others fit juvenile justice features. Also to further place American military justice in context, our military system is compared with the efforts of other nations to regulate and control deviant behavior in the military.

PHILOSOPHICAL AND JURISDICTIONAL APPROACHES

Military justice lies in the continuum between criminal and juvenile justice. It has features of both systems as well as its own unique attributes. Three features stand out in sketching these systems: (1) philosophical underpinnings, (2) nature of law and offenses, and (3) duration of state intervention.

Criminal and Juvenile Justice

A primary function of criminal justice is the protection of society from internal threats. The system is punitive in orientation. It acts against individuals held accountable for acts that society disapproves. Each of the states and the federal government has criminal law systems based on legislative and appellate court pronouncements. A basic principle of criminal law is that no act is punishable unless specifically and precisely defined in advance of its commission. Laws are drafted with each element of the offense closely defined. This norm is intended to promote clarity and certainty in law, giving adults reasonable notice of those acts to avoid and allowing criminal justice officials clear authority to intervene. The system reacts formally to previous culpable transgressions. Individuals are officially punishable for what they have done rather than who they are. The state provides predetermined, definite time constraints within which criminal justice may act, hold, and punish the deserving offender based on the nature and seriousness of the offensive conduct.

Juvenile justice is based on an ideology of social work. Its intent is to take a therapeutic approach, ostensibly operating on behalf of minors who are held to lesser degrees of responsibility than adults for the consequences of their acts. Children are defined as being immature, a personal condition that designates a state of incompetency. Their engagement in unacceptable behavior triggers governmental intervention. The state responds as if it were a parent offering solicitious custodial care under a parens patriae doctrine (Kittrie, 1980). The paternalistic state substitutes its will for these *incomplete* persons, and intrudes with the intention of being helpful and protective, seeking to treat the individual's condition so as to restore full development (Rubin, 1979).

Juvenile law is also rooted in statute and decisional law. It is designed to be a tool of benevolence, to be used to help the child become law-abiding. Although criminal codes target a relatively small chunk of potential conduct and define it as criminal, delinquency legislation encircles a much larger area of juvenile behavior. Delinquency statutes not only include offenses that would be illegal if committed by adults, but also encompass conduct illegal only for children, such as smoking, drinking, unwed motherhood, and curfew violations. These acts that have no counterparts in criminal law are termed "status offenses." Some of these status offenses lack the definitiveness of criminal law. Truancy, incorrigibility, ungovernability, or "leading an idle, dissolute or immoral life" are examples. These omnibus statutes, worded in ambiguous terms, allow government officials to cast a larger, looser discretionary net over children.

The juvenile justice system, concerned with the amelioration or correction of some personal dysfunction, is grounded in more forward-looking considerations than is criminal justice. The treatment-rehabilitation ideal cements the foundation of this justice system. Past behavior is viewed as an indicator of a troublesome state of being. The state's reaction is to impose open-ended assistance to change the minor to an improved status (Kittrie, 1980). The approach does not allow for a predetermined ceiling on intervention, except that juvenile law suggests that improvement is seemingly achieved automatically upon reaching the fixed year of majority (Cohen, 1980).

Military Justice

The goal of the military is to protect society from external threats. To accomplish its mission, the military maintains a relationship to its personnel that has been described as being "whole-life." It surrounds and touches them daily (Bernard, 1976). Military officers, practicing a kind of "professional paternalism" toward their subordinates, foster an ideology that the military is taking care of the individual (Radine, 1977: 56). In a sense, servicemembers are in a custodial relationship to the military, not unlike that of children in some form of parental custody. The military is an achievement-oriented subculture that encourages intimate control over its members. Military justice mirrors the norms and values of this environment.

The system of justice that has developed in the military is paternalistic and conciliatory as well as adversary and punitive. It offers training, education, discipline, and punishment. Minor offenders are judged to have made errors in judgment based on their lack of life experience and military socialization. The justice system is designed to give them a second chance to adjust to the military by informally processing them (Bernard, 1976). Violators are reprimanded, mildly sanctioned, and retrained. Major offenders are considered losers and are given up in the hope of preventing others from engaging in misconduct. Many are formally subjected to judicial proceedings. Upon conviction, they are invariably expelled from further service as well as subjected to long, predetermined, prison terms. Military justice then uses two divergent approaches toward violators: one centered on correction and the other on punishment.

Military law consists of federal statutes, presidential orders, service regulations and court decisions. Article 1 of the U.S. Constitution gives Congress the authority to make rules governing the armed forces. The present basic law is the Uniform Code of Military Justice (UCMJ) passed by Congress in 1950. The UCMJ is incorporated into title 10 of the United States Code. Its various articles define illegal conduct, establish court-martials, and outline the basic procedures in military justice. The UCMJ gives the President, as commander in chief, the power to promulgate additional procedures to implement the UCMJ. These procedures have been published in the *Manual for Courts-Martial* (MCM, 1969). In turn, each service has the latitude to develop specific regulations governing their personnel in conformity to the UCMJ and MCM. Finally, appellate court interpretations by the U.S. Supreme Court, and the Court of Military Appeals (COMA, the supreme court of the military), and each service's intermediate appellate court (Courts of Military Review, CMR) have interpreted the UCMJ and other rules.

Military law reflects dualities. There are offenses listed in the UCMJ articles and service regulations that one finds in any criminal or juvenile codes such as murder and robbery. Like delinquency legislation in the various states, however, military law identifies status offenses. Military law includes misbehaviors that are specifically applicable to servicemembers because of their occupational status as military personnel, such as AWOL, desertion, disobedience of an order, dereliction of duty, and haircut regulations. Some of these status offense prohibitions are precisely defined; others are vaguely worded and overly broad in scope. Perhaps the offenses that have been most often attacked are those in the general articles of the UCMJ: Article 133 prohibits "conduct unbecoming an officer and a gentleman"; Article 134 makes punishable "all disorders and neglects to the prejudice of good order and discipline in the armed forces, [and] "all conduct of a nature to bring discredit upon the armed forces." These two articles have an open-ended flavor to them. They are not readily understandable, a factor also present with juvenile status offenses. These military articles appear to prohibit almost any conduct that might displease a commanding officer (Bernard, 1976). Just as it has been argued that any child could be judged a status violator for almost any behavior (Gough, 1980), one can also argue that any servicemember risks exposure to the great breadth of military status offenses. Attacks in the appellate courts under the void for vagueness doctrine largely have been defeated in both systems (Gough, 1980; Parker v. Levy, 1974). Appellate cases analyzing these articles only affirm what is being punished. They offer little direction for what may be punished in future cases (Bernard, 1976). The result is that soldiers as well as children are subject to more stringent control than are adult civilians.

The assumptions and even the language underpinning the jurisdictional rationales of juvenile and military justice are remarkably similar for offenses unique to both settings. Each is concerned with promoting obedience to lawful authority, and, at the same time, to lessen personal freedom and independence of action. Both involve heavily affirmative action from members subject to either system. An omnibus character permeates juvenile and military justice absent for the most part in criminal justice. If commands of parents or military authorities are not followed—or, more seriously, are defied—then the social good to be achieved in each context will be lessened. The essence of status offense jurisdiction, as so many statutes illustrate, is the reinforcement of filial control (Schultz and Cohen, 1980). The need is to maintain "discipline" in the family (State of West Virginia ex rel., 1977) or the military by standardizing behaviors. Juvenile laws encompass refusals to submit to lawful and reasonable commands of parents, guardians, or school authorities (Rubin, 1979). The difference between lawful demands of parents and lawful orders of military superiors (UCMJ, articles 90 and 91) is not that great. Indeed, juveniles have been processed for refusals to bathe regularly or do household chores (Gough, 1980). Similar acts have been punished under military law such as appearing in a dirty uniform, or failing to empty a wastebasket (General Accounting Office, 1980). In neither control system is there much scrutiny to examine closely the reasonableness of such commands. Chargeable juvenile offenses include failure to stay home—an act sometimes called desertion—or truant behavior at school, called unauthorized absence (Rubin, 1979), with petitions specifying the number of days the minor deserts or absents himself from his assigned place (State of West Virginia ex rel., 1977). Those adjudged juvenile or military status offenders are even treated alike. Both may be institutionalized among others who have committed acts seen as criminal by adult standards.

OVERVIEW OF MILITARY COURTS

Structure

The hierarchical structure of military courts is similar to that of criminal courts. The way some military courts operate, however, suggest important analogies with juvenile courts. Military courts are organized from narrow to increasingly broad jurisdiction. The court system is divided into two subsystems: nonjudicial and judicial. These subsystems are differentiated from each other by the degree of legal training required for decision making, the rules governing decision making, and the role functions of participants. In turn, within these subsystems are six levels, distinguished by procedures and penalties. The levels correspond not, as in criminal justice, to the seriousness of the offenses of which they have jurisdiction, but to the severity of the punishments they may impose (Mayers, 1981). Collectively, these levels form a continuum of procedural formality and sentencing authority (Asher, 1979). Each of these six levels will be briefly outlined and discussed in depth in this section.

At the bottom of the six-leveled structure is a nonjudicial subsystem that commonly handles minor offenses. It has three prongs: (1) nonpunitive measures, (2) article 15 proceedings, and (3) summary court-martials, the lowest trial court. These are administrative and disciplinary mechanisms that give wide discretion to military authorities. Many of the procedures and penalities at these levels are as informal as those existing in juvenile justice, particularly at the intake stage. To protect against abuse of discretion, the sanctions that may be imposed are strictly limited, and servicemembers—just as juveniles—are given the right to opt out of the nonjudicial subsystem and demand judicial processing under most circumstances. Nonjudicial responses are frequently sought when the evidence is so weak that the military would fail at judicial proceedings.

The judicial subsystem is composed of three trial courts that, in terms of procedures and partipants, have a greater resemblance to criminal courts than to juvenile ones. These military courts are adversary in nature, follow strict rules of evidence, and offer similar defenses to crime such as insanity. They also offer accused statutory rights that civilian adult defendants have under the U.S. Constitution. For example, there are Sixth Amendment equivalent rights to notice of the charges (UCMJ, article 35), confrontation of adverse witnesses (UCMJ, article 39), compulsory process for obtaining favorable witnesses (UCMJ, article 46), assistance of defense counsel (UCMJ, Article 27), and to a speedy and public trial (UCMJ, articles 10 and 33). At the same time, however, there are other rights guaranteed civilians that are not only denied military defendants, but young people as well. With few exceptions, individuals processed by juvenile courts in most states have no right to trial by jury (McKeiver v. Pennsylvania, 1970), to indictment by grand jury, or to bail (Rubin, 1979). These same rights are also withheld to military personnel. The Fifth Amendment to the U.S. Constitution expressly excepts military personnel from indictment by grand jury.[1] The Supreme Court has denied service personnel the right to trial by jury (O'Callahan v. Parker, 1969). The Court of Military Appeals (COMA) has ruled that bail is not available in the military (Horner v. Resor, 1970).

A part of the six-level subsystem, the three judicial courts consist of two intermediate and one superior court. The intermediate tribunals conduct two types of special court-martials: (4) straight specials and (5) bad conduct discharge specials. These are courts that can sentence an accused to up to six months confinement. The most salient sentencing difference between these two courts is that the latter is authorized to punitively discharge an offender. Punitive separations are punishments unique to military justice. Finally, at the top is the (6) general court-martial, a judicial forum that may punish an accused with any sentence authorized by law, including life imprisonment and death. A conviction at these three court-martials is considered a federal conviction for a criminal offense (General Accounting Office, 1980).

Whether nonjudicial or judicial, all court-martials are temporary trial forums. Military courts, as ad hoc tribunals, come into existence only after commanders authorized to convene courts order them to adjudicate particular cases. A judicial court has criminal jurisdiction. Its decisions are binding on federal courts (UCMJ, article 76). Nevertheless, these military courts, as congressional creations under article 1, U.S. Constitution, are not part of the federal judiciary (article 3 courts); their rulings are not subject to direct review by federal civilian courts (Burns v. Wilson, 1953); and they have no power to adjudge civil remedies. A court-martial is a federal tribunal, however, at least for double jeopardy purposes. Servicemembers cannot be tried in both a federal court and in a court-martial for the same act. Successive prosecutions by both a court-martial and a state court are governed by the same rules that apply to prosecutions in a state court and a federal district court (Everett, 1973).[2]

Participants

Nonjudicial fact-finding and sanctioning powers are conferred on one decision maker, a commissioned officer. This officer is not a lawyer. Except for summary court-martials, commanding officers of an unit or an installation are authorized to officially initiate the action, and to impose the punishment without trial. The one-to-one relationship between government authority and violator is unique. There isn't any workgroup, as is the case in juvenile or criminal courts. The legally untrained officer is a combination prosecutor, judge, and defense counsel. The arrangement is based on a view of the government authority as functioning in a paternal or avuncular role (Bernard, 1976).[3] Again, the closest parallel to this situation is found in juvenile justice with the role played by probation officers during intake.

Unlike the nonjudicial subsystem, a courthouse workgroup consisting of legally schooled judges, defense counsel, and prosecutors are required in the judicial subsystem. These workgroup members are part of a service's Judge Advocate General's Corps (JAG). JAG is responsible for satisfying the legal needs of a service. JAG officers are assigned a variety of duties for specified periods of time during their military service (Kornbluth, 1980). Over the course of their careers, JAG officers may be involved in prosecution, defense, contract, procurement, defense, administrative, and judicial work.[4] The rotational system encourages greater commitment to the military organization than to professional legal responsibilities (Radine, 1977). Other than JAG officers, the only decision-making participants are civilian defense counsel, military jurors, and commanders.

Those called prosecutors have limited responsibilities. They prepare the government's case and then argue it in court. Only commanders authorized to convene court-martials have power to initiate a prosecution. Prosecutors are within the chain of command of those officers who convene courts. Prosecutors' future ratings and career prospects are dependent on the recommendations of these commanders.

Defense counsel is typically a military or civilian lawyer. Civilian counsel may represent servicemembers at any court-martial at their own expense. Servicemembers, however, have a right to have military defense counsel at judicial proceedings irrespective of their financial status, or the seriousness of the offense charged. As a result, most servicemembers are represented only by military defense counsel. Until recently, military defense counsel were accountable to the installation command structure. It was as if public defenders were working out of the district attorney's office (Goodrich, 1982). In the Army and Air Force, these military attorneys are now under the direct supervision of an independent defense service. The separate organizational structure promotes autonomy of counsel, encouraging greater counsel loyalty to the interests of their clients and lessening the perception of accused that military counsel ultimately serve the interests of the military (Mayers, 1981; Spilker, 1980-1981).

Military judges have fact-finding and sentencing authority. Their powers are similar to those of civilian judges in federal court. They can hold pretrial hearings, rule on motions, consider challenges to court members (jurors), and direct a judgment of acquittal. These judges also make all rulings on questions of law and they generally administer trials. Important differences exist, however, between military and civilian judges. One difference is that military judges do not have a fixed term or tenure. They are subject to transfer to nonjudicial duties at almost any time. Another difference is that they have fewer sentencing options and aids. Military judges are not the sentencing authority when military juries are sitting (UCMJ, article 51). Even when the accused elects to be tried and sentenced by military judge alone, military judges cannot place a servicemember on probation or suspend a sentence. Only commanders have that authority (U.S. vs. Occhi, 1976). In making their decisions on sentencing, they do not have the benefit of a presentence investigation report. They must rely upon the evidence submitted during the sentencing stage of the trial.

A third difference is their relationship to the military structure and the command initiating the prosecution. Military judges are part of the executive branch of government; however, civilian judges are members of a co-equal branch of the government. Presiding over general court-martials, military judges are members of an independent judiciary established within each of the services. This judiciary is organizationally outside the local command (Kadish et al., 1980). Judges presiding over special courts, on the other hand, are within the immediate chain of command (Everett, 1973). This creates an impression among servicemembers that these lower court judges are not completely insulated from command pressure (Moyer, 1970).

Finally, fact-finding and sentencing may be done by the military's functional equivalent to jurors, court members.[5] Court members are also part of the installation's chain of command. Commanders select court members to serve at trial from among their officers or, if requested by the defendant, from enlisted personnel. In cases in which enlisted members are requested, at least one-third of total court membership must be from enlisted ranks (USMJ, article 25). A random method of court member selection is not required. Commanders choose those they believe are best qualified by reason of age, education, training, experience, length of service, and judicial temperament (UCMJ, article 25). In almost all jury cases the accused is from the enlisted ranks and the court-members are officers. In the rare requests for enlisted members, senior noncommissioned officers (NCOs) are selected. Career NCOs have a reputation for making even harsher judgments than officers. The service length necessary to become court members indicates that they have become socialized in military thinking, and actually represent a relatively homogeneous group (Heil, 1982). Servicemembers, as a result, do not benefit from a court member tribunal with a wide range of attitudes and backgrounds, representing a cross-section of their community. Nor are they tried by their peers (Rinaldi, 1973). By giving commanders power to hand-pick members, some have suggested that the jury has been stacked (Radine, 1977). This may help to explain why trial by court members is less common than trial by judge alone.

In determining the verdict, court members must unanimously agree if the death penalty is mandatory by law. In all other cases, the concurrence of two-thirds of those voting is required to convict the accused (UCMJ, article 52). A vote of less than two-thirds is an acquittal, not a hung jury. Although the Supreme Court has held that unanimity is not constitutionally required for conviction (Apodaca v. Oregon, 1972), federal law and most state courts require a unanimous verdict to convict. The sentencing authority given to court members differentiates the military system from the federal and most state jurisdictions. Sentencing is usually a judicial function outside military justice. A unanimous vote is required for a sentence of death; three-fourths for confinement over ten years; and two-thirds for lesser sentences.

Whether members of separate organizations or not, those who participate in the military courthouse—except for civilian counsel—are military personnel. Servicemembers are interested in career advancement. Their courthouse duties require allegiance to legal principles. The military environment exalts strict obedience to authority and the achievement of military objectives. Military personnel, as a result, are subject to role tensions. Some of those who do not conform may fear some form of retaliation (Everett, 1973). Others are subject to subtle pressures and overt harassments (West, 1977). Most courthouse participants, however, do not experience conflict because their views are congruent with those of the military (Radine, 1977).

One participant that has not been discussed fully is the commander. Throughout the nonjudicial and judicial subsystems, commanders are important decision makers. Their powers and role functions, unknown to other justice systems, require a separate discussion.

Role of Commanders

Unique to military justice is the role of the commander. Despite having very little training in law, commanders have broad discretion over military justice in keeping with the military concept that commanders have ultimate responsibility for the servicemembers under their control (Hodson, 1975). They decide when and what to chastise or punish. Processing begins and is completed, subject to appellate review, with the actions taken by these officers. Depending on their rank and duty status, these officers have supervisory authority over many facets of middle stage processing.[6]

The initial decision to do something to an alleged violator is a command decision (Kadish et al., 1980). In nonjudicial actions other than a summary courts-martial, a commander may play judicial, prosecutorial, and defense role. Court-martial charges are preferred by commanders. Court-martials themselves are convened by a commander in the accused's chain of command.[7] As convening authorities, commanders, under present law, detail the judge (article 26), trial, and defense counsel (article 27), and court members (article 25) to court-martials.[8] Once the court is convened, commanders do not have the authority to overtly influence the court. They are prohibited by the UCMJ from attempting to control judicial proceedings or personnel (UCMJ, articles 37 and 98). But less blatant ways of influencing the court do occur (Radine, 1977; West, 1977).

Upon conviction, commanders take final action on cases. Commanders automatically become the reviewing authority of court-martials. They must be satisfied beyond a reasonable doubt that the findings are supported by the evidence (UCMJ, articles 60 and 64). They may either approve the action of the courts or take action in favor of the accused by disapproving the findings or sentence of the courts. This may reduce any punishment adjudged. The sentence approval authority of commanders means that plea bargaining is formally conducted between convening authorities and defendants. Several types of pretrial agreements may be made. In return for a guilty plea, a convening authority may reduce the charged offenses, or may withdraw the remaining charges, thereby lowering the ceiling on the potential maximum sentence (Gray, 1978). The most frequent type of pretrial agreement is one in which the convening authority agrees to approve no sentence in excess of that agreed upon. Sentence bargains are therefore guaranteed.[9]

The powers conferred on commanders require that they have multiple roles—that quite obviously conflict. Nevertheless, the military has argued successfully for the maintenance of these powers, though statutory and administrative changes in recent years have lessened some of them (see Military Justice Acts of 1983 and 1968). Military authorities argue that commanders need such omnipresent control over military justice so that they can control their troops. But the assertion has never been empirically tested.

MILITARY COURT PROCESSING: PROCEDURAL LEVELS

Nonjudicial

Nonpunitive measures. At the bottom of the list of measures are the nonpunitive measures. These are administrative actions that include extra training, transfer in assignment, denial of privileges, criticisms, and elimination from service. Criticisms refer to censure, admonition, and reprimand. The two marine commanders in Beirut at the time of the 1983 truck bombing of the Marine compound were considered for reprimands or admonitions. These are letters that would be inserted in their personnel file, becoming part of their performance evaluation and would effectively prevent any further promotions (Byrne, 1981; St. Louis Post Dispatch, 1984).

An administrative discharge is the most severe nonpunitive measure. The services have a right to terminate a person's military career whenever it is determined that such a member is unqualified for retention (Comptroller General of the United States, 1980). Under "discharge for the good of the service in lieu of trial," for example, servicemembers charged with a serious offense may be terminated with their consent. From 1967 to 1976, more than 150,000 service personnel received this discharge. The character of the discharge given in almost all cases is "under other than honorable conditions," the most severe form of administrative discharge (Comptroller General of the United States, 1978). Critics have asserted that this discharge character is a "badge of infamy" that seriously interferes with employment opportunities and eligibility for veterans benefits. More important, the public appears to equate this discharge character with a court-martial conviction and punitive discharge, a discharge given only by a court-martial that brands servicemembers as dishonorable (Effron, 1974; Lasseter and Thwing, 1982). Administrative discharge proceedings offer much less procedural protections than that of any court-martial. Because an accused may be quickly processed, it is used often by military authorities. It proves to be an effective substitute for a court-martial, avoiding the safeguards found in trial courts, and at the same time imposing economic and social liabilities on servicemembers (Asher, 1979).

Article 15. This article of the UCMJ authorizes the imposition of punitive measures for military law violations without the intervention of trial proceedings.[10] Article 15 is designed to deal with minor offenses—that is, offenses analogous to civilian misdemeanors in which imprisonment is limited to a maximum of one year. There is, however, no legal bar to using article 15 punishments for offenses that would be considered felonies in civilian life (Capella v. United States, 1980). The analogue often applied to justify use of article 15 is that of a commanding officer who wants to correct a young person's behavior in the same manner as a father taking his son out to the "woodshed" for punishment (Bernard, 1976). Nevertheless, the way the services use article 15 belies such a benign characterization.

Article 15 punishment is not considered a court-imposed penalty. Maximum penalities for officers include arrest in quarters for 30 days and forfeiture of the equivalent of one month's pay. But rarely do officers receive article 15 punishment (Radine, 1977). On the other hand, enlisted members are open to more severe punishments. They may receive 60 days' restriction, 45 days' extra duties, reduction in rank up to two pay grades, forfeiture of one month's pay and 30 days' correctional custody. In the Navy, article 15 punishment may consist of solitary confinement on bread and water for three days when the accused is attached to or embarked on a vessel (UCMJ, Article 15 [b] [2] [A]). Correctional custody, although not technically confinement, is physical restraint that has been viewed as being very much like incarceration in jail (Rivkin and Stichman, 1977).[11]

Beyond these immediate punishments, receipt of an article 15 punishment may result in serious, long-term legal and administrative sanctions. A record of nonjudicial punishment may be used to (1) increase the severity of court-martial sentences, [12] (2) justify a less-than-honorable discharge, (3) show unsuitability for government service and civilian employment, (4) create prison records for service women confined in federal correctional institutions,[13] (5) permanently threaten promotion and retirement,[14] and (6) deny duty assignments (Salisbury, 1982). These outcomes undercut the notion of the military as the "parent" interested only in assisting the erring servicemember to adjust to military life.

Nonjudicial punishment is not given automatically in most circumstances.[15] Servicemembers may decline any article 15 punishment, or, in contesting their case, attempt to persuade the commander either that they do not deserve any punishment or, if punishment is appropriate, that they deserve only minimum sanctions. Those who refuse to submit to punishment are exposed to the possibility that the commander may then seek the preferring of court-martial charges.[16]

Punishment may be imposed without any formal hearing. An informal, nonadversary hearing is required in most circumstances. Article 15 sessions are held before those commanding officers who have the power to impose nonjudicial punishment. At these hearings, servicemembers must be informed of the charge. They have a right to present evidence in defense, extenuation, or mitigation (MCM, paragraphs 133a and 133b). Servicemembers may also call witnesses in defense, request the proceedings be open to the public, and have a person represent their interests. The representative, however, need not be an attorney. Servicemembers do not have a right to counsel (Middendorf v. Henry, 1976). Neither servicemembers not their agents may question or cross-examine witnesses except if the commanding officer grants such a request. They do not have any compulsory process available for obtaining witnesses. The rules of evidence need not be followed. If the commander is "convinced" that the accused committed the offense, the commander then can impose punishment (Department of the Army Regulation c-18, 27-10, 1979).

Appeal of the punishment is to the next highest officer in the chain of command.[17] Cases under appeal may be executed. Few servicemembers appeal their case because if they were likely to appeal, they would have originally turned down the article 15 punishment (Radine, 1977). Servicemembers also do not appeal punishment because they doubt the integrity of the appeal process, and see little chance of success (General Accounting Office, 1980). Imposition of an article 15 punishment is not a bar to court-martial for that same offense (UCMJ, article 15 [f]; see U.S. v. Joseph, 1981; U.S. v. Fretwell, 1960).[18] Because servicemembers are exposed to a dual punishment track, they cannot escape a kind of double jeopardy (Goodrich, 1982).

An article 15 proceeding is the workhorse of military justice (Rivkin and Stichman, 1977). For every 1978 court-martial in the armed forces for example, more than 16 nonjudicial punishments were administered (General Accounting Office, 1980). An article 15 punishment can be administered rather quickly and simply at an informal hearing. It requires less time and personnel than trial by court-martial. When jurisdictional defects prevent the military from court-martialling an accused, it is often used (Salisbury, 1982). As a result, commanders use nonjudicial punishment as an attractive, frequently used weapon for dealing with violators.

Summary courts. A summary court-martial is the lowest trial court level with the fewest legal formalities. It is an administrative rather than a judicial proceeding (Middendorf v. Henry, 1976). A simplified proceeding, it is equivalent to a police court in civilian jurisdictions (Salisbury, 1982). The jurisdiction of the court is restricted. It cannot try any capital offense. Nor can officers be tried, raising an equal protection argument. Punishment imposed here cannot exceed confinement for 30 days, hard labor for 45 days, restriction for two months, forfeiture of two-thirds pay for one month, or reduction to the lowest grade.[19] Although the punishments are relatively light, conviction at a summary court, under certain circumstances, can be used to aggravate the sentence imposed at a later special or general court-martial (MCM, paragraph 127c).

Consistent with the rules governing article 15, enlisted servicemembers can be tried at this level only with their consent. If servicemembers object to trial by summary court-martial, trial by a higher court may be ordered. Although defendants have greater due process protections at a higher court level, vulnerability to receiving a more severe punishment is increased.[20]

The defendant does not have a statutory right to the appointment of military counsel at a summary court (UCMJ, article 27, 38[b]; MCM, paragraph 79d). The U.S. Supreme Court in *Middendorf v. Henry* (1976) characterized the summary court as not an adversary, punitive proceeding, but rather a disciplinary one that did not result in a "criminal conviction," and held that no Sixth Amendment right to counsel attaches to summary courts.[21]

Servicemembers are not tried by a professional jurist. They are tried by a commissioned officer who typically does not have a legal background (UCMJ, article 16). The officer assigned to the case is expected to perform judicial, fact-finding, prosecutorial, and defense duties, roles that inherently conflict (Goodrich, 1982). Defendants may cross-examine witnesses, testify, and present evidence. Although the rules of evidence do apply (MCM, paragraph 137), the trial record need not disclose anything of the factual or legal basis of the finding.[22] No direct appeal is allowed to either a court of military review or the Court of Military Appeals (UCMJ, articles 66[b] and 67[b]). Direct appeal is to the officer who convened the summary court only. The officer who convened the summary court may review, suspend, or vacate the sentence (MCM, paragraph 88), and his or her superior may do the same (MCM, paragraph 94).

Criticisms of summary courts are abundant. Commanders are said to use summary courts when they have weak evidence and only are concerned with immediate punishment. The possibility of command influence also is increased because the person making the accusation can convene the court and choose the presiding office (MCM, paragraph 5c). Its one-officer court has been viewed as creating a "kangaroo court" (Radine, 1977: 188). Congress has thought about its use for years, but has declined to abolish it (Asher, 1979).

Judicial

Special courts. A special court-martial is an intermediate level court. It deals with those accused who commit what in the civilian justice system would be considered lesser felonies and misdemeanors (Kadish et al., 1980). A high volume of cases are processed here. It is the "workhorse" of the court-martial subsystem. Special courts have the authority to try any case involving noncapital offenses as well as, under certain circumstances, capital offenses other than spying (UCMJ, article 19; MCM, paragraph 15). There are two types of special court-martial, "straight" specials and bad conduct discharge special court-martials (BCD special). A straight special is a lesser court than a BCD special. A straight special can impose confinement for not more than six months, hard labor for not more than three months, restriction, forfeiture of two-thirds pay for not more than six months and reduction to the lowest enlisted grade (UCMJ, article 19). A BCD special can impose these same punishments, and, in addition, can punitively discharge the accused with a bad conduct discharge (UCMJ, article 23). The BCD discharge is given to those who have committed serious military status or criminal offenses.

Greater procedural requirements are needed at a BCD special than at a straight special. At both specials, an accused may be tried by judge alone or court members. If servicemembers do not request trial by judge alone, they will be automatically tried by court members. At least three members are required to proceed to trial by court members. A BCD special must be presided over by a trained military judge. The only exception to this requirement is made because of "physical conditions or military exigencies" (UCMJ, article 19). In such cases, the president of the court—who is the highest ranking member—presides. Special courts, however, are rarely held without a military judge (Bishop, 1974). Both a prosecutor and lawyer defense counsel are appointed to a BCD special (UCMJ, article 27). The BCD special accused has the same rights to a qualified attorney as a GCM defendant. The straight special accused is entitled to trained military counsel, however, unless such trained counsel is unavailable.[23] A formal record of the proceeding, a complete and verbatim transcript, must only be made in a BCD special (UCMJ, article 19). Review of straight special accused is by the convening authority and the JAG officer. If a bad conduct discharge is adjudged, then an automatic appeal to the Court of Military Review takes place (UCMJ, article 67).

General Courts. A general court-martial (GCM) is the highest trial forum in military law. Its jurisdiction extends to any person subject to the UCMJ for any offense made punishable by the code. A GCM may impose any sanction not prohibited by military law up to and including death. Lesser punishments include a dishonorable or bad-conduct discharge or a dismissal for officers. Civilians charged with committing war crimes also may be tried by GCM (UCMJ, article 18, MCM, paragraph 14).

The GCM offers the most procedural protections prior to and during the trial. Before the GCM can be convened certain steps must be followed. A legal opinion as to the disposition of the charges must be given to the convening authority. The written advice is given by the staff judge advocate, a convening authority's chief legal counsel (UCMJ, article 34). Although seldom done, a convening authority may take action contrary to the staff judge advocate's recommendation (Kadish et al., 1980).

Cases that are referred to a GCM must first be reviewed at a hearing called an article 32 investigation (UCMJ, article 32; MCM, paragraph 34). The objective of this hearing is to provide convening authorities with information that will help them to decide how to dispose of the charges (Kadish et al., 1980). This hearing has been traditionally compared to a grand jury proceeding required under federal law and in some states (Moyer, 1972). Both are used to determine whether a person is brought to trial. Nevertheless, unlike a grand jury that consists of from 12 to 23 members, an article 32 is composed of one commissioned officer. The individual selected by the convening authority to be the article 32 investigating officer (IO) is required to be an impartial and mature officer (MCM, paragraph 34a). Also, both federal and state grand jury proceedings are carefully kept secret, and the accused and the defense counsel are excluded (Moyer, 1970). In contrast, article 32 proceedings are generally open, defendants are present, and defendants have a right to representation by appointed military lawyer counsel or, if they prefer, by hired civilian counsel. Defendants may also confront or cross-examine witnesses, present evidence, and may speak for themselves. Nevertheless, the rules of evidence do not apply (U.S. v. Weaver, 1962). Although from the defendants' perspective article 32 investigations may be favorably compared to a grand jury, in reality, it is very much like a preliminary hearing that has one judge and in which the accused participates and attends. An important difference, is that decisions by a grand jury or preliminary hearing judge are binding on a prosecutor; however, they are not in the military. The article 32 IO may only recommend action for or against referral to trial to the convening authority. The convening authority may disregard without comment the IO's recommendation (MCM, paragraph 35). An article 32 investigation then cannot be an effective screening device.

At the trial, a trained military judge must preside and rule on questions of trial procedure and admissibility of evidence. A complete trial record must be made. The accused has a right to the appointment of trained military defense counsel, to civilian counsel (at the accused's own expense) or military counsel of their own selection if such counsel is reasonably available (UCMJ, article 38[b]). A GCM tried by court members must consist of five or more members. A GCM conviction is reviewed by the convening authority and the defendant's legal officer. The Court of Military Review will automatically review sentences involving a punitive discharge or confinement over one year (UCMJ, article 67).

MILITARY JUSTICE: ALTERNATIVE SYSTEMS

Military justice is certainly different from criminal justice in many important respects. At the same time, it bears some striking resemblances to juvenile justice. Both juvenile and military justice have not been immune to calls for change and reform. Juvenile justice has come under increasingly heavy attack in recent years for a variety of reasons. Critics believe that status offense laws cover too broad an area of behavior, giving juvenile courts too much responsibility for operating effectively. The vagueness of status offenses is under attack by those who argue that such laws violate the juvenile's rights to know precisely what is forbidden. Suggestions have been put forward that status offenders should be removed from juvenile court jurisdiction because of the detrimental effects of labeling a child as a lawbreaker, the ineffectiveness of courts in dealing with status offenders, and the severe disposition given to them (Teitelbaum and Gough, 1977). At the same time, a related avenue of attack focuses on the due process rights of juveniles. Some want to give juveniles the same rights provided to adults. Others focus on legal problems at particular stages. For example, some believe that the imposition of informal probation at a nonjudicial hearing is an infringement of a juvenile's constitutional rights (Krisberg and Austin, 1978).

Reform of military justice has been difficult and gradual, but no less intense than those efforts to change juvenile justice. Each congressional change of the UCMJ has been an attempt to root out the appearance or reality of evil in military justice. Over the years, many of the changes wrought have resulted in the system becoming more closely aligned with criminal justice. That may not be evident in the presentation above. But in comparison with the past—a history not explored here—military justice today is more like civilian, especially federal, justice systems.

Despite changes, major problems with the system have been identified. There have been calls to abolish court-martial jurisdiction over all civilian-type offenses, transferring criminal type cases from the military to the civilian courts (Younkins, 1978). Others have advocated the complete abolition of the court-martial for offenses committed within the United States (Sherman, 1973). A related view argues that the military judicial system should be run by civilian administrators under the control of the United States attorney general. Civilian trial attorneys and civilian judges should occupy the roles now filled by military legal officers (West, 1977). The intent behind these reforms is the desire to guarantee the full participation of servicemembers in the enjoyment of all legal rights and protections accorded civilian adults. But military authorities resist all such proposals. They suggest that "military necessity" requires a separate system of justice. The military, they argue, "is a society apart from civilian life which requires different legal standards the civilian courts cannot appreciate or enforce" (Sherman, 1973: 1401). Three reasons have been advanced for a separate system: (1) the desire for quick and summary ways for maintaining discipline; (2) the need for military expertise in adjudicating military status offenses (Goodrich, 1982); and (3) the fact that military units are stationed overseas (Hodson, 1975). These points are, on the face, quite reasonable. Nevertheless, an examination of the experiences of other nations weakens the American military's argument.

We are one of the few Western nations that has not either abolished or dramatically reformed its military justice system. France generally abolished its court-martial system in 1982. French military judicial courts cannot be convened in peacetime within the country itself. Only in times of war or national crisis may the military try servicemembers within France. Outside of the country, military justice retains total control over its servicemembers (Darfren, 1983). In West Germany, all offenses committed by servicemembers are tried by civilian courts. The only exceptions are those offenses committed abroad, on a navy vessel, or during wartime (Krueger-Sprengel, 1972). Sweden's court-martial system comes into existence only during wars or emergencies. Military offenses have been added to the civilian criminal code, but made applicable only to servicemembers. Servicemembers who commit offenses overseas are returned to Sweden for trial in civilian courts (Lindeblad, 1963). What these nations have in common is that they have abolished the judicial subsystem, yet retained the nonjudicial one, allowing the military the ability to respond swiftly, but not too severely, to offenses committed by servicemembers. Servicemembers in these countries, for the most part, enjoy the rights provided to any citizen. Other nations, although not abolishing their judicial systems, have increased the role played by civilians in court-martials. In the United Kingdom, for example, judges are civilians (McBrien, 1983).

In solving one's own problems, knowledge of the experiences of others frequently is of great value. Too often our responses to problems are colored by our cultural experiences so that what is possible is defined within narrow parameters. If we would like to see our servicemembers treated like other citizens, we should examine the feasibility of adapting the models provided by other nations to improving the quality of justice in our armed forces. Our commitment should be guided by our desire to see all servicemembers treated as first class citizens in uniform.

NOTES

1. The fifth amendment states that no person shall be held to answer for a capital or otherwise infamous crime, unless on a presentment or indictment of a grand jury, except in cases arising in the land or naval forces, or in the militia, when in actual service in time of war or public dangers.

2. Also, in contrast to federal courts, the place of military trial is not determined by where the alleged offense occurred (MCM, paragraph 8; U.S. v. Lahman, 1981).

3. Commanders are authorized to act swiftly against violators, to efficiently treat misbehaviors, to instill discipline and obedience in their troops, and to maintain overall control over their units.

4. This is a "ticket punching" personnel system that JAG officers must go through to enhance their prospects for promotions. The rotational system insures that JAG officers become generalists rather than specialists in any one branch of military law.

5. Although these court members have many duties that are the same as civilian jurors, they are not considered jurors, as COMA has ruled that an accused facing trial by court-martial is not entitled to jury trial under the UCMJ (U.S. v. Kemp, 1973).

6. Commanders may authorize searches, or order into arrest or pretrial confinement a servicemember under their authority (UCMJ, article 9). They can also initiate any judicial or nonjudicial proceeding after they receive information indicating that a member under their command committed an offense under the UCMJ (Kadish et al., 1980).

7. Some commanders have summary court-martial convening authority; others exercise either special or general court-martial jurisdiction. If special court convening authorities believe that the offenses are so serious that general court-martials may be appropriate, they must appoint commissioned officers to conduct investigations (UCMJ, articles 32 and 34). When officers exercising general court-martial jurisdiction receive reports of the investigations and the subordinate convening authorities' recommendations, they may dismiss the charges or take action to initiate the processing of cases at one of the six procedural levels identified earlier. For example, they may return the charges to proper subordinate commanders for trial by lesser court-martials.

8. Effective August 1, 1984, however, convening authorities will be personally responsible only for detailing the court members (Military Justice Act of 1983).

9. If the court sentences an accused to five years and the agreement is only for three, for example, then the reviewing authority approves the three-year sentence. Interestingly, if the agreement is for three years, and the court gives the accused two, then the reviewing authority must approve the two-year sentence. An accused who plea bargains receives two chances for leniency.

10. Article 15s are called "Office Hours" in the Marine Corps and "Captain's Mast" in the Navy and Coast Guard.

11. This form of custody is normally served in a minimum security area apart from other prisoners. A servicemember may be required to undergo extra duties, fatigue duties, or hard labor while in correctional custody. Although the purposes of correctional custody are to deter illegal conduct and provide rehabilitative service, it has a reputation in the Navy for severe discipline (Salisbury, 1982).

12. An article 15 offense may be introduced during court-martial sentencing as evidence of aggravation. It stands as proof of the defendant's prior service record of misconduct, as evidence of bad character, and is treated as if it were like a court-martial conviction (MCM, paragraphs 76a [2], 76d; see U.S. v. Booker, 1978).

13. Navy enlisted women, for example, have served correctional custody in federal penitentiaries because the Navy lacks facilities for them. The booking procedures used at these federal facilities result in their receiving federal records. Copies of these records are forwarded to the FBI, also creating a national arrest record (Salisbury, 1982).

14. A single article 15 offense may ruin or terminate a career of an officer in the competitive military profession today.

15. Servicemembers cannot refuse an article 15 punishment if attached to or embarked in a vessel. The vessel exception has been vigorously attacked by critics as an unwarranted denial of equal treatment for shipboard servicemembers (Salisbury, 1982). The exception is designed to protect a ship's captain with a small complement of officers from meeting the requirements for a minimum number of officers to serve at a court-martial. Treating servicemembers differently on all vessels has been questioned for large ships on which a captain has a sufficient number of officers to convene a court and "he, rather than the accused, wants a trial" (Salisbury, 1982: 867). Further, attachment to a vessel has been interpreted with the widest possible scope, and includes those who are not even on or near their ships. Attachment may be shown in any number of ways. For example, having orders to the ship, using the vessel's fleet post office address to receive mail, or being subject to recall to the vessel are each sufficient to establish attachment. A result is that a sailor is attached to a vessel even though the ship is in drydock for over a year, or is thousands of miles away (Salisbury, 1982).

16. Servicemembers facing the dilemma between submission to an article 15 punishment and court-martial are provided with the assistance of counsel in making that choice. (General Accounting Office, 1980). Failure to provide counsel, or to waive the right to consult with counsel, acts as a bar to the admissibility of the article 15 punishment in any way at any subsequent court-martial except when servicemembers are attached to a ship (U.S. v. Booker, 1978; U.S. v. Mack, 1980).

17. This commander may refer the appeal to a military attorney for an examination of the record. The attorney, however, does not have the authority to mitigate the sentence (MCM, paragraph 135). Nevertheless, some federal district courts have reviewed appeals (See Bennett v. Tarquin, 1979) and the Court of Claims will hear cases if punishment affects pay and allowances (See Hagarty v. U.S., 1971; Capella vs. U.S., 1980).

18. Nonjudicial punishment for a minor offense, however, cannot be tried later (MCM, paragraph 68a).

19. Senior enlisted personnel cannot receive any form of confinement, hard labor, or reduction, except to the next inferior grade (UCMJ, article 20; MCM, paragraph 16[b].

20. To assist servicemembers to make a better informed choice between these two options, they are offered the opportunity to confer with or waive advice of counsel. Failure to meet this requirement prevents the results of the summary court from being used against them in any way at a subsequent court-martial (U.S. v. Booker, 1978).

21. In *Middendorf v. Henry* (1976), Justice Rehnquist reasoned that summary courts were like parole revocation hearings in which the Supreme Court already had held that no Sixth Amendment right to counsel exists (Gagnon v. Scarpelli, 1973). But servicemembers may still retain a civilian lawyer at their own expense, and the military often provides free military counsel. Counsel is mandatory at trial, however, if the summary conviction is subsequently used at a latter tribunal to impose a stigmatizing discharge. Summary defendants without defense counsel cannot have the conviction used against them for issuing a punitive discharge at a subsequent court-martial unless the defendants knowingly waive counsel (U.S. v. Booker, 1978).

22. The record is limited to the charges, pleas, findings, sentence, approval of convening authority, and the consent of the accused to trial by summary court-martial.

23. If unavailable, the accused is entitled to counsel with at least as much formal training as the prosecuting counsel. At least the Army, however, commonly does provide for the appointment of a military defense counsel and for a military judge to preside at a straight special.

CASES

APODACA v. OREGON (1972) U.S. 404 (1972)
BENNETT v. TARQUIN (1979) 466 F. Supp. 257 Hawaii
BREED v. JONES (1975) 421 U.S. 519
BURNS v. WILSON (1953) U.S. 137
CAPELLA v. UNITED STATES (1980) 624 F. 2d 976 Ct. Cl.
GAGNON v. SCARPELLI (1973) 411 U.S. 778
HAGARTY v. UNITED STATES (1971) 449 F. 2d 352 Ct. Cl.
HORNER v. RESOR (1970) 19 C.M.A. 285, 41 C.M.R. 285
McKEIVER v. PENNSYLVANIA (1970) 430 U.S. 528
MIDDENDORF v. HENRY (1976) 425 U.S. 25
MIRANDA v. ARIZONA (1966) 384 U.S. 436
O'CALLAHAN v. PARKER (1969) 395 U.S. 258
PARKER v. LEVY (1974) 417 U.S. 733
SANTOBELLO v. NEW YORK (1971) 404 U.S. 257
UNITED STATES v. BOOKER (1977) 3 M.J. 443, reversed in part, 5 M.J. 246 (1968)
UNITED STATES v. FRETWELL (1960) 11 C.M.A. 377, 29 C.M.R. 193
UNITED STATES v. JOSEPH (1981) 11 M.J. 333
UNITED STATES v. KEMP (1973) 22 C.M.A. 152, 46 C.M.R. 152
UNITED STATES v. LAHMAN (1981) 12 M.J. 513 (NMCR)
UNITED STATES v. MACK (1980) 9 M.J. 300
UNITED STATES v. OCCHI (1976) 2 M.J. 60
UNITED STATES v. WEAVER (1962) 13 C.M.A. 147, 32 C.M.R. 147

REFERENCES

ASHER, S. E. (1979) "Reforming the summary court-martial." Columbia Law Review 79(1): 173-197.

BERNARD, K. S. (1976) "Structure of American military justice." University of Pennsylvania Law Review 125(2): 307-336.

BISHOP, J. W. (1974) Justice Under Fire. New York: Charterhouse.

Bureau of the Census (1980) 1980 Census of Population. Washington, DC: Government Printing Office.

BYRNE, E. M. (1981) Military Law. Annapolis, MD: Naval Institute Press.

COHEN, F. (1980) "Juvenile offenders: proportionality vs. treatment," pp. 363-370 in T. H. Rubin (ed.), Juveniles in Justice. Santa Monica, CA: Goodyear.

Comptroller General of the United States (1978) Report to the Congress of the United States: Eliminate Administrative Discharges in Lieu of Court-Martial: Guidance for Pleas Agreements in Military Courts is Needed (FPCD-77-48). Washington, DC: General Accounting Office.

———(1980) Report to the Congress of the United States: Military Discharge Policies and Practices Result in Wide Disparities: Congressional Review is Needed (FPCD-80-13). Washington, DC: General Accounting Office.

DARFREN, M. (1983) "Armee de terre." Defense Nationale (March): 155-158.

Department of the Army Regulation C-18 (1979) Military Justice. Washington, DC: Legal Services.

Department of Defense (1981) Defense '81—Special Almanac Issue. Arlington, VA: American Forces Information Service.

———(1983) Defense '83—Special Almanac Issue. Arlington, VA: American Forces Information Service.

EFFRON, A. S. (1974) "Punishment of enlisted persons outside the UCMJ." Harvard Civil Rights-Civil Liberties Law Review 9: 227-324.

EVERETT, R. O. (1973) "The new look in military justice." Duke Law Journal 3: 649-701.

General Accounting Office (1980) Better Administration of the Military's Article 15 Punishments for Minor Offenses is Needed. (FPCD-80-19). Washington, DC: Author.

GOODRICH, C. (1982) "Denying soldiers the rights they fight to protect." California Lawyer (November): 48-53, 79.

GOUGH, A. R. (1980) "Beyond-control youth in the juvenile court—the climate for change," pp. 118-146 in T. H. Rubin (ed.), Juveniles in Justice. Santa Monica, CA: Goodyear.

GRAY, K. D. (1978) "Negotiated pleas in the military," Federal Bar Journal 37(Winter): 49-60.

HEIL, G. M. (1982) "Military triers of fact," Hastings Law Journal 33: 727-753.

HODSON, K. J. (1975) "Military justice: abolish or change." Military Law Review 27-100(September): 579-606.

KADISH, M. J., G. B. ROBERTS, J. F. ROMANO, and R. S. KADISH (1980) "Representing the military defendant." Trial 16(10): 50-57.

KITTRIE, N. (1980) "The divestment of criminal law and the coming of the therapeutic state," pp. 141-156 in F. Cohen (ed.), The Law of Deprivation of Liberty. St. Paul, MN: West.

KORNBLUTH, J. (1980) "JAGS: the army's gung ho lawyers." The American Lawyer (July): 34-36.

KRISBERG, B. and J. AUSTIN (1978) The Children of Ishmael: Critical Perspectives on Juvenile Justice. Palo Alto, CA: Mayfield.

KRUEGER-APRENGEL, F. (1972) "The German military system." Military Law Review (57): 17-26.

LASSETER, E. F. and J. B. THWIG (1982) "Military justice in time of war." American Bar Association Journal 57: 17-26.

LINDEBLAD, B. (1963) "Swedish military jurisdiction." Military Law Review 19: 123-128.

Manual for Courts-Martial, United States (1969) Executive Order 11476. Washington, DC: Government Printing Office.

MAYERS, L. (1981) The American Legal System. Littleton, CO: Fred B. Rothman.

McBRIEN, E.J.D. (1983) "An outline of British military law." The Military Law and Law of War Review 22(1-2): 9-48.

Military Justice Act of 1983, P. L. 98-209 (1983) Amendment to Title 10, U.S.C. Code, Uniform Code of Military Justice.

Military Justice Act of 1968, P.L. 90-632 (1968) Sections 1-4, 82 Stat. 1335.

MOYER, H. E. (1970) "Procedural rights of the military accused: advantages over a civilian defendant." Maine Law Review 22: 105-140.

RADINE, L. B. (1977) The Taming of the Troops. Westport, CT: Greenwood.

RINALDI, M. (1973) "The olive-drab rebels." Radical America 8: 16-52.

RIVKIN, R. S. and B. F. STICHMAN (1977) The Rights of Military Personnel. New York: Avon.

RUBIN, T. H. (1979) Juvenile Justice: Policy, Practice, and Law. Santa Monica, CA: Goodyear.

SALISBURY, W. R. (1982) "Nonjudicial punishment under article 15 of the United States Code of Military Justice." San Diego Law Review 19: 839-875.

SCHULTZ, J. L. and F. COHEN (1980) "Isolationism in juvenile court jurisprudence in pursuing justice for the child," pp. 612-629 in F. Cohen (ed.), The Law of Deprivation of Liberty. St. Paul, MN: West.

SHERMAN, E. F. (1973) "The civilianization of military law." Maine Law Review 22: 3-103.

SPILKER, A. J. (1980-1981) "The ethical charge to counsel." The Air Force Law Review 22(2): 101-119.

St. Louis Post Dispatch (1984) "Reprimands urged for command laxity in Beirut." January 1: 8A.

State of West Virginia ex. rel. Harris v. Calendire, 233 S.E. 2d 318 (1977) pp. 147-156 in T. H. Rubin (ed.), Juveniles in Justice. Santa Monica, CA: Goodyear.

TEITELBAUM, L. E. and A. R. GOUGH (1977) Beyond Control. Cambridge, MA: Ballinger.

TROJANOWICZ, R. C. and M. MORASH (1983) Juvenile Delinquency: Concepts and Control. Englewood Cliffs: NJ: Prentice-Hall.

Uniform Code of Military Justice (1950) Title 10, U.S.C. Sections 801-940, Articles 1-140.

WEST, L. C. (1977) They Call It Justice. New York: Viking.

YOUNKINS, P. R. (1978) "Divergent trends in military law." Rutgers Law Review 31(4): 759-785.

6.

PROTECTING DEFENDANTS' RIGHTS:
A Review of Literature on State and Federal Courts

Jack E. Call
University of Nebraska

In an often cited article entitled "The Myth of Parity," law professor Burt Neuborne (1977) discusses at length the issue of whether state or federal courts should be favored as forums for the resolution of legal issues relating to the assertion of individual rights. As an experienced civil liberties lawyer, it is Neuborne's (1977: 1116-1117) judgment that "persons advancing federal constitutional claims against local officials will fare better, as a rule, in a federal rather than a state trial court."

The purpose of this chapter is to evaluate that judgment based upon an assessment of the relevant evidence found in the legal and social science literature on courts. The general question addressed is: Which are more liberal—state or federal courts?[1] Nagel (1963: 29) defined liberalism as "a viewpoint associated with the interests of the lower or less privileged economic or social groups in a society." It is consistent with the values associated with Packer's due process model, in which the emphasis is on protecting the defendant's right to equal treatment and minimizing errors in the criminal process, even if the result is a more inefficient process (Packer, 1968). Conversely, conservatism is defined as "a viewpoint associated with the interests of upper or dominant groups in a society" (Nagel, 1963: 29). It is consistent with the values associated with Packer's crime control model, where the emphasis is on the creation of a quick and efficient criminal process (Packer, 1968). Although defendants' rights remain important under this model, a presumption of guilt is attached to a defendant when enough evidence exists to hold him or her for a crime. The term "moderate" will be used to describe positions that fall between these two points of view.

Although the question of the relative liberalism of state and federal courts is perhaps most relevant in civil cases—in which a party has a choice as to whether to file a complaint in state or federal court—it is nevertheless an important question for students of the criminal justice system as well. Its relevance derives from the nature of the relationship between state and federal courts in criminal cases. In criminal cases the defendant has no choice as to whether his or her case will be tried in a state or a federal court. The judicial forum depends upon whether the defendant's actions violated state or federal criminal law. However, state criminal codes are much more comprehensive than the federal criminal code, so the vast majority of criminal cases are tried in state courts.

Nevertheless, a federal court eventually rules on constitutional issues raised in a substantial number of state criminal cases. The review occurs when the defendant in a state case files a writ of habeas corpus in federal court, typically alleging that he or she is being incarcerated illegally because of an improper conviction. The usual allegation is that one or more of the defendant's constitutional rights were violated during the course of the trial. An important question in these cases is whether the defendant's allegations are more likely to be resolved in the defendant's favor in state or federal courts.

This is not simply an academic question. The right of defendants to seek review of their cases in federal court by means of a writ of habeas corpus is a right created by federal statute. Consequently, Congress can restrict or eliminate the right by modifying the habeas corpus statute. In making such a decision, Congress might find it relevant to ask whether state or federal courts are more supportive of individual rights (i.e., more liberal).

In addition, federal courts (most important of which is the Supreme Court) must interpret the habeas corpus statute and thereby determine the extent of the right provided by the statute. For example, recently the Supreme Court held in *Stone v. Powell* (1976) that federal courts need not relitigate search and seizure issues in a habeas corpus proceeding after the defendant has had the opportunity to litigate those issues fully in state court. There was considerable speculation that the Court would expand the reasoning used in *Stone v. Powell* to limit the relitigation of other criminal procedural issues in federal habeas corpus proceedings as well. Thus far this expansion has not occurred. However, the habeas corpus statute does not provide a clearcut answer to the question of whether to expand the reasoning in Stone v. Powell.

In such "close" cases, the Court often considers the effects of the alternatives available to it. Like Congress, the Court might find it relevant to consider whether individual rights are more likely to be supported in state or federal courts.

Thus the question of whether state or federal courts are more liberal should be of interest to students of the criminal justice system. Consequently, although all studies providing relevant evidence on the question of the relative liberalism of state and federal courts have been included in this chapter, particular attention will be given to those studies dealing with criminal justice issues. The first section marshals the relevant evidence found in five bodies of literature on courts. The second section discusses the conclusions that can be drawn fairly from this evidence. In the last section, limitations on the utility of the evidence are explored.

MARSHALLING THE EVIDENCE

For the most part, neither the social science nor the legal literature has been very interested in whether judicial output is liberal or conservative. However, a large portion of both bodies of literature has focused on judicial output in one way or another. As a result, many of the studies in these two areas developed data from which reasonable inferences can be made about whether the judicial output under study was relatively liberal or conservative. These studies fall into five general categories: (1) descriptive empirical studies, (2) judicial role literature, (3) judicial compliance literature, (4) literature on the expanding role of state courts, and (5) empirical studies comparing federal and state court output.

Descriptive Empirical Studies

The seventeen studies in this category vary greatly in their primary focus. However, they are all empirical in that they involve a systematic examination of cases rather than an examination of only "leading" cases or some other group of cases selected subjectively.

Thirteen of the seventeen studies looked at state courts and provide some evidence that state courts are at least moderate and in some instances are somewhat liberal. The greatest evidence of liberal leanings is provided by two studies of worker's compensation cases (Ulmer, 1962; Stecher, 1977). Ulmer found that all ten of the judges serving on the Michigan Supreme Court from 1958 to 1950 voted for the claimant in worker's compensation cases in at least half the cases. Stecher examined 961 worker's compensation cases from selected periods between 1945 and 1972. In all five states she studied, the percentage of cases decided in favor of the claimant exceeded 50 percent.

Other studies provide evidence of moderate postures on the part of state appellate courts (Galie, 1979; Vitiello and Burger, 1981; Levin, 1977; Comment, 1977; Kagan et al., 1977; Tarr and Porter, 1982). For example, during the period 1940-1970, Kagan and his colleagues found that in eight of sixteen states studied, the percentage of pro-defendant decisions exceeded 35 percent.[2] Stecher (1977) found that three of the five state supreme courts she studied had pro-defendant percentages in criminal cases of 40 percent or more. Galie (1979) found that the New York Court of Appeals was at least as liberal as the U.S. Supreme Court on criminal procedural issues in the 1960s and 1970s. Vitiello and Burger found a surprising willingness on the part of state appellate courts to exclude evidence that was allegedly obtained unconstitutionally, ranging from 13 percent in homicide cases to 40 percent in drug cases.

There was some evidence of state court conservatism as well. Nagel (1962) found low pro-defendant percentages in criminal cases decided in 1955 by the Pennsylvania and New Jersey Supreme Courts (22 percent and 25 percent, respectively). McGovern (1981) found that about two-thirds of the 29 state supreme courts ruling on the constitutionality of statutes of repose (statutes restricting the period in which product liability suits may be brought) upheld the statutes.

The four descriptive empirical studies of federal courts also paint a moderate picture. Richardson and Vines (1970) studied the decisions of district courts in three federal circuits from 1956-1961. In labor cases, most of the judges were moderately liberal, but in civil liberties cases most of the judges were generally conservative. In another study, Vines (1963) found evidence of liberalism in three circuit courts of appeals, in which 75 percent of the circuit courts' race-related decisions in cases arising in southern states from 1956-1961 favored the black party in the case. When Vines analyzed the district court cases in these same states during the same time period, he found that over half of those cases were decided in favor of the black party. However, he also concluded that in 48.7 percent of the cases decided against the black party "the relevant higher court precedents pointed toward a larger proportion of Negro victories" (Vines, 1963: 314). In the fourth federal court study, Walker (1972) found evidence of moderate conservatism in the federal district courts. In a random sample of 1177 civil liberties cases decided between 1963 and 1968, 38.3 percent of the cases were decided in favor of the civil liberties claim.

One descriptive, empirical study devoted part of its attention to a comparison of state and federal court output. Tarr and Porter (1982) examined state and federal court treatment of constitutional claims of gender discrimination in interscholastic athletics. They found that federal courts were more inclined to require mixed participation in non-contact sports whereas state courts were slightly more likely to prohibit exclusion of women from contact sports.

On the whole, the descriptive empirical studies suggest that both state and federal courts are at least moderate. However, much of the evidence is ambiguous in that it indicates some state courts are liberal and others are conservative; many of the studies are based on a small number of cases, and many of the studies are based on data that is at least twenty years old.

The evidence provided by these studies as to criminal cases is limited to state courts. It suggests a considerable range in posture from state to state. Of particular interest, however, are the findings by Kagan et al. (1977) that eight of sixteen state supreme courts studied had pro-defendant percentages in excess of 35 percent; by Stecher (1977) that three of five state supreme courts studied had pro-defendant percentages of 40 percent or more; and by Vitiello and Burger (1981) that state appellate courts have demonstrated a substantial willingness to exclude illegally-obtained evidence in criminal cases. These findings suggest that state courts are at worst somewhat more receptive to the claims of criminal defendants than traditional expectations would have suggested.

Judicial Role Literature

Judicial role studies hypothesize that a judge's perceptions of the norms and expectations attached to the status occupied by a judge can be used to predict or explain a judge's decisions (Sheldon, 1974). Only two judicial role studies provide some evidence about the relative liberalism of state and federal courts.

Glick (1971) found evidence of moderate state court conservatism on the supreme courts of Louisiana, New Jersey, Pennsylvania, and Massachusetts in the late 1960s. In criminal, tax, employee injury, auto accident, and business liability cases, the liberal voting percentage was 38.3 percent.

Howard (1977) analyzed over 5700 votes in cases from 1965-1967 in three federal circuits. His data suggest that these federal courts were moderately liberal. The liberal voting percentage exceeded 50 percent in income tax, labor-management, patent, copyright, civil rights, and employee injury cases. However, in prisoner petitions and criminal cases the liberal voting percentage dropped below 30 percent.

Howard (1977) concluded from this differential that a judge may be a liberal in one area and a conservative in another. However, there is another possible explanation: It seems likely that criminal and prisoner petition cases raise proportionately fewer meritorious issues than other types of cases. It is likely that the proportion of criminal cases that are appealed exceeds the proportion of civil cases appealed because most criminal defendants are indigent and are entitled to free appointed counsel for one appeal. Thus, it costs such defendants nothing to appeal. Similarly, prisoners are provided free legal assistance or legal resources to assist them in appealing their convictions or in bringing civil rights claims. In such circumstances the only cost to prisoners is their time, a commodity that they possess in abundance. In other types of cases, however, the appealing party asserts its claim only at considerable financial cost. The result in such cases is that less meritorious claims are filtered out and not appealed because the costs are judged to be too high in comparison to the chances for success on appeal. Thus, a 30 percent liberal voting percentage in criminal and prisoner petition cases may well be comparable to a 50 or 60 percent liberal record in other subject areas.

Although the evidence provided by these two judicial role studies suggests that federal courts are more liberal than state courts, such a conclusion cannot be drawn with confidence from only two studies. In addition, the data in the studies are somewhat dated. On the other hand, both studies examined a large number of cases.

Judicial Compliance Literature

Judicial compliance studies focus on the extent and manner in which lower courts comply with the mandates of the Supreme Court. For our purposes, the term will be expanded slightly to include studies that examine the reactions to or treatment of Supreme Court decisions by lower courts.

The compliance literature provides a special kind of evidence about the relative liberalism of courts. Nearly all the compliance studies have analyzed the reactions of lower courts to Warren Court decisions that invariably are ground-breaking liberal decisions—such as *Mapp v. Ohio* (1961), which made the exclusionary rule binding on the states, or *Miranda v. Arizona* (1966), which required the police to give warnings to suspects in custody about the right to counsel and the right to remain silent during interrogation. Consequently, if the lower courts are conservative, a substantial amount of noncompliance by those courts would be expected. On the other hand, failure to find such non-compliance does not mean necessarily that the lower courts studied are liberal. Compliance could simply mean that the obligation felt by the lower courts to comply with the pronouncements of the highest court in the land exceeded the courts' desire to make what they would have considered wiser and fairer decisions by evading the Supreme Court's holdings. However, it is often easy to avoid unpopular precedents, so in all likelihood compliance with liberal Warren Court decisions is an indication of at least moderation on the part of lower courts.

The compliance studies have examined state court reactions more than federal court reactions. The state court compliance studies suggest that state courts are moderately conservative, but the evidence is far from overwhelming.

On the conservative side, Romans (1974) examined state supreme court decisions between 1958 and 1968 that involved confessions. Roman's purpose was to examine that impact of *Escobedo v. Illinois* (1964) and Miranda on the liberalism of state supreme courts. These two cases restricted dramatically the authority of police to conduct custodial interrogations of suspects without providing them access to counsel and without advising them of their right to remain silent. He found that only 29 percent of the state supreme courts were liberal after Miranda.

Lefstein et al. (1969) studied three large urban juvenile courts after In re Gault (1967), which required juvenile courts to extend to juveniles a number of procedural rights that had been thought previously to be applicable only to adult criminal defendants. They found a rather startling reluctance on the part of the fifteen judges and referees studied to comply with Gault. For example, they found that two of the courts almost never gave full advice as to the juveniles' right to counsel, including a right to appointed counsel if they were indigent. Even when partial advice was given, it was usually given quite rapidly with little concern as to whether it was understood or in such a way as to encourage waiver of the right. Similarly, they found that in one court juveniles were never advised of their right to remain silent. In another court, they were advised in only 29 percent of the cases, and again the advice given was almost always prejudicial advice.

Gruhl's study (1981) of all state supreme court decisions from 1971-1978 dealing with the implications of Miranda also found evidence of moderate conservatism. Miranda held that confessions obtained during custodial interrogation without first giving the suspect several "warnings" about right to counsel and right against self-incrimination could not be used in evidence against the suspect at a subsequent trial. However, in only 19 percent of the cases did the state courts disallow the use of illegally obtained statements to impeach the defendant's testimony at trial. In only 49 percent of the cases did the state courts disallow the use of confessions obtained after incorrect Miranda warnings were given. In only 57 percent of the cases were confessions disallowed even though they had been obtained during interrogation that took place after the defendant had requested an attorney or had asked to be allowed to remain silent. Only in the fourth area examined by Gruhl did the state courts show evidence of moderation: In 75 percent of the cases the state courts did not allow the prosecution to impeach a defendant's testimony at trial by pointing out that the defendant had refused to answer police questions.

Other compliance studies of state courts show some evidence of moderation. Beatty (1972) studied 199 state court decisions overturned by the Supreme Court in the period from 1959 to 1969 and relitigated in state courts. In only 18 cases did the state courts act in an evasive or quasi-evasive manner.[3] Canon (1974) studied more than 1800 state court cases citing Mapp, Escobedo, Miranda, or Gault from 1961 to 1972. In only 90 cases did the state court react in a manner that he characterized as constituting "organizational contumacy." He described organizational contumacy as either a categorical refusal by lower courts to comply with a Supreme Court decision or as compliance "in a dramatically begruding [sic] fashion with no appearance of routineness" (Canon, 1974: 53). In another study, Canon (1973) examined state court treatment of sixteen questions left unanswered by Mapp. He found that nine states gave Mapp a broad reading, but nine other states gave it a narrow reading.[4] Tarr (1977) examined 98 state supreme court decisions from 1947 to 1973 involving construction of the Religious Establishment Clause in the First Amendment. He found only 13 cases failed to apply Supreme Court decisions properly.

The studies of compliance by federal courts suggest a moderate stance. Gruhl (1980) studied lower federal court treatment of libel cases in the decade after *New York Times v. Sullivan,* 1964, which made it more difficult for public officials to win libel suits. He found extensive compliance with the *New York Times* decision as well as a substantial tendency to extend the decision before the Supreme Court did so. Johnson (1981) analyzed citations of Warren Court civil liberties decisions by federal appellate courts during the latter years of the Warren Court and the early years of the Burger Court. He found high percentages of positive citations of liberal Warren Court decisions during both periods. Even Peltason's classic study (1961) of southern federal judges in the period just after *Brown v. Board of Education* (1954) provides surprising evidence of moderation. Of the 36 judges who were discussed enough to permit their evaluation, 20 complied largely with Brown under circumstances of great public pressure toward noncompliance. In the only conservative finding, Murphy (1959) found that federal courts in the District of Columbia between 1956 and 1958 admitted confessions in 16 of 21 cases in which the confession was obtained during a delay in arraignment—in spite of a Supreme Court decision that seemed to call for a different result.

One compliance study makes a direct comparison of state and federal court performance. Gruhl (1982) analyzed the treatment of libel cases by federal appellate courts and state supreme courts. He found that both groups of courts complied with the decision in *New York Times* in over eighty percent of the libel cases they decided. The only significant difference between the performance of the two groups of courts was that the federal courts were substantially more likely to extend the holding in *New York Times* before the Supreme Court did so.

The compliance literature suggests that federal courts are somewhat more liberal than state courts. However, the difference does not appear to be very great, and its significance is diminished by the fact that evaluation of the relative liberalism of federal courts is based on rather sparse evidence. The evidence in the criminal justice area related almost entirely to state courts. The Romans (1974), Lefstein et al. (1969), and Gruhl (1980, 1982) studies provide strong evidence of state court conservatism; however, the two Canon (1974, 1979) studies reveal moderation by state courts. On the federal court side, only the Murphy (1959) article examined a criminal justice issue, but the evidence it provides is too fragmentary to permit a meaningful comment about the posture of federal courts in criminal cases.

Literature on the Expanding
Role of State Courts

In recent years a large body of literature has concluded that the state courts increasingly are using state constitutional provisions to circumvent conservative decisions by the Burger Supreme Court, particularly in the area of individual rights.[5] However, as a source of evidence about the liberalism of state courts, these studies suffer from a serious shortcoming—they do not discuss state court decisions on a particular subject as a whole. Instead, they usually point out only remarkable, ground-breaking decisions so that the overall posture of the states on the subject cannot be determined. Nevertheless, this literature is important because two significant generalizations can be drawn from it:

(1) The majority of state supreme courts have rendered at least one important recent liberal civil liberties decision. In a comprehensive work, the Harvard Law Review staff cited 29 states as having rendered "aberrational cases that extend various rights beyond the dictates of federal law in the area of criminal procedures" (Developments in the Law, 1982). Hancock (1982) listed 24 state courts that have interpreted criminal procedural safeguards in their state constitutions more liberally than Supreme Court interpretations of similar provisions in the U.S. Constitution. Her list included three states not included in the *Harvard Law Review* list. In another law review note, 23 states were listed as having rendered liberal civil liberties decisions since 1960 (Project Report, 1973). This list added four more states to the *Harvard Law Review* list. Thus it can be stated with confidence that state courts in at least 36 states have issued liberal civil liberties opinions since 1960.

(2) The majority of state courts are not liberal on civil liberties issues as a whole. The evidence in support of this generalization is not precise. However, the following comment is repeated in similar form in many of the articles on the expanding role of state courts: "Any survey of state constitutional doctrine must begin by recognizing that state cases going beyond the federal floor remain the exception rather than the rule" (Developments in the Law, 1982: 1370).

The literature on the expanding role of state courts standing alone would not be very helpful for our purposes because it provides no information about federal courts. However, it is important because it suggests that state courts are not as conservative as the legal literature would seem to suggest. This conclusion is particularly relevant with respect to state court treatment of criminal justice issues. Several of the articles in this body of literature deal exclusively with criminal cases, and most of the remaining articles include important references to state court expansions of defendants' rights.

Comparative Quantitative Literature

Only two of the studies in the sections above explicitly compared state and federal court performance. However, in the Tarr and Porter (1982) study the primary focus was not on the comparative aspect of the study. Therefore, the Gruhl study (1982) and the four studies discussed below represent the only studies to date, the explicit purpose of which is to compare quantitatively state and federal court treatment of substantive legal issues.

Vines (1965) studied civil rights cases in southern state supreme courts and federal district courts during the decade after *Brown v. Board of Education*. Only 29.2 percent of the civil rights cases decided by southern state supreme courts during the period were decided in favor of the black party to the case. Southern federal district courts decided over half (51.3 percent) of the civil rights cases it heard in favor of blacks. Although Vines discovered considerable variation among the southern state supreme courts, the pro-black disposition rate in several state supreme courts exceeded that of the federal district courts in the state.

Beiser (1968) studied reapportionment cases during the two years following the Supreme Court's landmark decision in *Baker v. Carr* (1962) accepting jurisdiction over reapportionment cases. Examining 29 federal and 19 state apportionment cases, he tested five hypotheses in which the state courts were viewed as likely to be more critical of the Supreme Court's decision, narrower in their interpretations of the decision, or less forceful in their enforcement of it. One hypothesis could not be tested quantitatively. As to the other four hypotheses, there were some differences between state and federal court reactions but none were statistically significant. Furthermore, the direction of the differences was not always consistent with the hypothesis.

Grunbaum and Wenner (1980) examined all cases reported in the Environmental Reporter Cases (ERC) through mid-1977. The authors hypothesized that state courts would be more favorably disposed toward business and less favorably disposed toward environment issues, but neither hypothesis was supported by the data. State courts were more likely than federal courts to decide a case in favor of the environmental interests. They were also less pro-business than federal courts, but the difference was not statistically significant.

Hass (1981, 1982) examined all the published opinions of state supreme courts and federal courts of appeals from 1969 to 1979 that dealt with one or more of nine issues concerning the right of inmates to access the courts. He found that federal circuit courts of appeals resolved more prisoner access questions than did the state supreme courts, that federal courts were more than twice as likely to decide prisoner access questions in favor of the prisoner, and that the state supreme court's opinions contained no more critical references to the Supreme Court than did the federal appellate court opinions.

These comparative, quantitative studies are mixed in their support of the traditional assumption that federal courts are more liberal than state courts. The studies by Hass (1981, 1982) and by Vines (1964, 1965) support the assumption. To a lesser extent, the Gruhl (1982) study is also supportive. The Grunbaum and Wenner (1980) study is inconsistent with the assumption. The evidence from the Beiser (1968) study is mixed. Thus the overall thrust of these five works is moderate support for the conclusion that federal courts are more liberal. Only the Hass article dealt specifically with criminal justice issues and it suggests that federal courts are more liberal.

EVALUATING THE EVIDENCE

Perhaps the most difficult aspect of answering the question of whether state or federal courts are more liberal is evaluating the evidence as a whole. The descriptive empirical literature suggests little difference between the two groups of courts: the judicial role, compliance, and comparative quantitative studies provide moderate evidence that federal courts are more liberal; the literature on the expanding role of state courts suggests that state courts are more liberal than suggested by traditional legal wisdom. However, all the groups of literature have important limitations. Many of the descriptive empirical studies have a small data base; others—the federal court studies, in particular—are based on rather old data. The contribution of the judicial role literature is based on only two relevant studies. In the compliance literature the evidence on federal courts is quite weak: two of the studies (Peltason, 1961; Murphy, 1959) are dated and one (Johnson, 1981) provides only indirect evidence about liberalism. The value of the literature on the expanding role of state courts is diminished because it provides no evidence at all about federal court performance.

In spite of these limitations, three general but necessarily tentative conclusions can be drawn from this literature as a whole: (1) the federal courts are somewhat more liberal than federal courts, (2) the gap between federal and state courts is not great, and certainly not as great as the legal literature would cause one to think, and (3) from all indications, the gap is closing.

These three tentative conclusions can also be made with respect to the relative liberalism of state and federal courts on criminal justice issues. However, the conclusions must be viewed with less confidence in this area because the studies provide very little evidence about the performance of federal courts in criminal cases. Nevertheless, one can conclude with confidence that there is substantial (and growing) evidence that state appellate courts are more inclined to rule favorably on issues raised by defendants in criminal cases than most observers of the courts would have expected.

NOTES

1. The term "more liberal" is used throughout the paper for consistency and ease of communication. Its use does not necessarily represent a judgment that courts should be more liberal.

2. In my judgment, most scholars of the judicial process would be impressed with pro-defendant percentages in excess of 35 percent in criminal cases. See the later discussion in the text of Howard's study (1977) for an explanation of this conclusion.

3. An evasive case was one in which the Supreme Court heard the case again and overruled the state court again. A quasi-evasive case was one in which Beatty and at least one dissenting state court judge thought that the second state court decision violated the Supreme Court mandate. Beatty has been criticized as having used too narrow a concept of evasion (Schneider, 1973).

4. The other states either fell into an intermediate category or defied characterization.

5. See Developments in the Law (1982: 1328-1329, footnote 20) for the most comprehensive list of literature. In addition to the 29 articles listed there, the following works should be added: Galie (1981, 1982), Notes (1978, 1979), Porter (1978), Mosk (1978), Williams (1983), Friedelbaum (1982), Harrison (1982), Hancock (1982), and Keeton (1969).

CASES

BAKER V. CARR (1962) 369 U.S. 186
BROWN v. BOARD OF EDUCATION (1954) 347 U.S. 483
ESCOBEDO v. ILLINOIS (1964) 378 U.S. 478
In re GAULT (1967) 387 U.S. 1
MAPP v. OHIO (1961) 367 U.S. 643
MIRANDA v. ARIZONA (1966) 384 U.S. 436
NEW YORK TIMES v. SULLIVAN (1964) 376 U.S. 254
STONE v. POWELL (1976) 96 S.Ct. 3037

REFERENCES

BAUM, L. and B. CANON (1982) "State supreme courts as activists: new doctrines in the law of torts," pp. 83-108 in M. C. Porter and G. A. Tarr (eds.), State Supreme Courts: Policymakers in the Federal System. Westport: CT: Greenwood.

BEATTY, J. K. (1972) "State court evasion of United States Supreme Court mandates during the last decade of the Warren Court. Valparaiso Law Review 6: 260-285.

BEISER, E. N. (1968) "A comparative analysis of state and federal judicial behavior: the reapportionment cases." American Political Science Review 8: 109-134.

CANON, B. (1973) "Reactions of state supreme courts to a United States Supreme Court civil liberties decision." Law and Society Review 8: 109-134.

———(1974) "Organizational contumacy in the transmission of judicial policies: the Mapp, Escobedo, Miranda, and Gault cases." Villanova Law Review 20: 50-79.

———and D. JAROS (1979) "The impact of changes in judicial doctrine: the abrogation of charitable immunity." Law and Society Review 13: 969-986.

Comment (1977) "Equal rights provisions: the experience under state constitutions." California Law Review 65: 1086-1112.

Developments in the Law (1982) "The interpretation of state constitutional rights." Harvard Law Review 95: 1324-1502.

FAIR, D. R. (1967) "An experimental application of scalogram analysis to state supreme court decisions." Wisconsin Law Review 1967: 449-467.

FRIEDELBAUM, S. (1982) "Independent state grounds: contemporary invitations to judicial activism," in M. C. Porter and G. A. Tarr (eds.), State Supreme Courts: Policymakers in the Federal System. Westport, CT: Greenwood.

GALIE, P. J. (1979) "State constitutional guarantees and protection of defendants' rights: the case of New York, 1960-1978." Buffalo Law Review 28: 154-194.

———(1981) "The Pennsylvania constitution and the protection of defendants' rights, 1969-80: a summary." *University of Pittsburgh Law Review* 42: 269-311.

———(1982) "The other supreme courts: judicial activism among state courts." *Syracuse Law Review* 33: 731-793.

GLICK, H. (1971) *Supreme Courts in State Politics: An Investigation of the Judicial Role*. New York: Basic Books.

GRUHL, J. (1980) "The Supreme Court's impact on the law of libel: compliance by lower federal courts." *Western Political Quarterly* 33: 502-519.

———(1981) "State supreme courts and the United States Supreme Court's post-Miranda rulings." *Journal of Criminal Law and Criminology* 72: 886-913.

———(1982) "Patterns of compliance with U.S. Supreme Court rulings: the case of libel in federal courts of appeals and state supreme courts." *Publius* 12(3): 109-126.

GRUNBAUM, W. F. and L. M. WENNER (1980) "Comparing Environmental Litigation in State and Federal Courts." *Publius* 10: 129-142.

HASS, Kenneth C. (1981) "The 'new federalism' and prisoners' rights: state supreme courts in comparative perspective." *Western Political Quarterly* 40: 552-571.

———(1982) "The Comparative study of state and federal judicial behavior." *Journal of Politics* 44: 721-746.

HANCOCK, C. (1982) "State court activism and searches incident to arrest." *Virgina Law Review* 68: 1085-1136.

HARRISON, R. S. (1982) "State court activism in exclusionary-zoning cases," pp. 55-82 in M. C. Porter and G. A. Tarr (eds.), *State Supreme Courts: Policymakers in the Federal System*. Westport, CT: Greenwood.

HOWARD, J. W., Jr. (1977) "Role perceptions and behavior in three U.S. courts of appeals." *Journal of Politics* 39: 916-938.

JOHNSON, C. A. (1981) "Do lower courts anticipate changes in Supreme Court policies?" *Law and Policy Quarterly* 3: 55-68.

KAGAN, R. A., B. CARTWRIGHT, L. M. FRIEDMAN, and S. WHEELER (1977) "The business of state supreme courts: 1870-1970." *Stanford Law Review* 30: 121-156.

KEETON, R. E. (1969) *Venturing To Do Justice: Reforming Private Law*. Cambridge, MA: Harvard University Press.

LEFSTEIN, N., V. STAPLETON, and L. TEITELBAUM (1969) "In search of juvenile justice: Gault and its implementation." *Law and Society Review* 3: 491-562.

LEVIN, B. (1977) "Current trends in school finance reform litigation: a summary." *Duke Law Journal* 1977: 1099-1137.

McGOVERN, F. E. (1981) "The variety, policy, and constitutionality of product liability statutes of repose." *American University Law Review* 30: 579-641.

MOSK, S. (1978) "Contemporary federalism." *Pacific Law Journal* 9: 711-721.

MURPHY, W. (1959) "Lower court checks on Supreme Court Power." *American Political Science Review* 53: 1017-1031.

——— (1962) "Testing relations between judicial characteristics and judicial decision-making." *Western Political Quarterly* 15: 425-437.

NAGEL, S. (1963) "Off-the-bench judicial attitudes," in G. Schubert (ed.), *Judicial Decision-Making*. New York: Macmillan.

NEUBORNE, B. (1977) "The myth of parity." *Harvard Law Review* 90: 1105-1131.

Note (1978) "Stepping into the breach: basing defendants' rights on state rather than federal law." *American Criminal Law Review* 15: 339-381.

Note (1979) "The independent application of state constitutional provisions to questions of criminal procedure." *Marquette Law Review* 62: 596-621.

PACKER, H. (1968) The limits of the Criminal Sanction. Palo Alto, CA: Stanford University Press.

PELTASON, J. (1961) *Fifty Eight Lonely Men*. New York: Harcourt Brace Jovanovich. University Press.

PORTER, M. C. (1978) "State supreme courts and the legacy of the Warren Court." *Publius* 8: 55-74.

Project Report (1973) "Toward an activist role for state bills of rights." *Harvard Civil Rights-Civil Liberties Law Review* 8: 271-350.

RICHARDSON, R. J. and K. VINES (1970) *The Politics of Federal Courts: Lower Courts in the United States*. Boston: Little, Brown.

ROMANS, N. T. (1974) "The role of state supreme courts in judicial policy making: Escobedo, Miranda and the use of judicial analysis." *Western Political Quarterly* 27: 38-59.

SCHNEIDER, R. (1973) "State court evasion of the United States Supreme Court mandates: a reconsideration of the evidence." *Valparaiso Law Review* 7: 191-195.

SHELDON. C. H. (1974) *The American Judicial Process: Models and Approaches*. New York: Dodd, Mead.

STECHER, J. (1977) "Democratic and Republican justice: judicial decison-making on five state supreme courts." *Columbia Journal of Law and Social Problems* 13: 137-181.

TARR, G. A. (1977) *Judicial Impact and State Supreme Courts*. Lexington, MA: D. C. Heath.

———and M. C. PORTER (1982) "Gender equality and judicial federalism: the role of state appellate courts." *Hastings Constitutional Law Quarterly* 9: 919-973.

ULMER, S. S. (1962) "The political party variable in the Michigan supreme court." *Journal of Public Law* 11: 352-356.

VINES, K. (1963) "The role of circuit courts of appeals in the federal judicial process: a case study." *Midwest Journal of Political Science* 7: 305-319.

———(1964) "Federal district judges and race relations cases in the South." *Journal of Politics* 26: 337-357.

———(1965) "Southern state supreme courts and race relations." *Western Political Quarterly* 18: 5-18.

VITIELLO, M. and J. C. BURGER (1981) "Mapp's exclusionary rule: is the court crying wolf?" *Dickinson Law Review* 86: 15-39.

WALKER, T. G. (1972) "A note concerning partisan influences on trial judge decision-making." *Law and Society Review* 6: 645-649.

WILLIAMS, A. Jr. (1983) "The new patrol for the accused: state constitutions as a buffer against retrenchment." *Howard Law Journal* 26: 1307-1334.

IV.

The Effect of Court Decisions on Administration of Criminal Justice

There are many studies of the impact of specific U.S. Supreme Court decisions. Analyses of the effect of Miranda v. Arizona and Mapp v. Ohio are, perhaps, most familiar to students of criminal justice. In these and other impact studies, researchers have demonstrated the limited effect of appellate court decisions, the symbolic character of the impact of the more controversial decisions, and the ways that lower courts and criminal justice agencies have modified or circumvented court mandates. In spite of the knowledge gained from this literature, we know very little about the imapct of trial court decisions and about the way appellate definition of doctrine constrains the administration of criminal justice. Few case studies have examined the way in which trial court decisions change or direct criminal justice processes, largely because such trial court decisions are relatively new. The best example of such intervention consists of federal district court decisions focusing on the management of local jails or state prison systems. There are few studies, however, that pertain to these decisions. Similarly, as most analyses of constitutional doctrine concentrate on developments in case law and not impact, there are few inquiries that direct attention to the impact of appellate doctrinal preferences on criminal justice agencies.

The two chapters in this section help to fill this void. Weber, Price and Perlman look at the implications of a consent decree issued by a federal district court in the Midwest. Focusing on jail overcrowding—a problem that has attracted the attention of numerous federal courts around the country—Weber and his colleagues analyze the effect of an injunction that set limits on jail population and mandated certain standards for the jail's administration. In this chapter, attention is directed to the impact of this single, federal district court decision.

The second chapter in this section concentrates on appellate court definition of doctrine. Examining the contemporary state of prisoners' rights, Cox and Speak argue against the doctrine of civil death and urge appellate courts to embrace a citizenship standard for corrections. The authors implicitly consider the effect of appellate court decisions when they examine the degree to which contemporary prisoners' rights correspond to either civil death or citizenship doctrines. They explicitly assume that appellate courts do impact corrections when they argue that the doctrine of universal citizenship has the strongest claim on both our legal tradition and the contemporary circumstances that constitute corrections.

FEDERAL COURT IMPACT ON
A LOCAL JAIL

Charles Weber
Albert C. Price
Ellis Perlman
University of Michigan—Flint

The impact of federal judicial decisions upon policies of state and local government has been substantial. Such far-reaching Supreme Court decisions as *Brown v. Board of Education* (1954), *Baker v. Carr* (1962), and *Miranda v. Arizona* (1966) changed the outcomes of the political system with regard to school segregation, legislative redistricting, and criminal procedure. More recently, federal district courts have involved themselves in disputes over prison and jail conditions (Harris and Spiller, 1976). This chapter, developed from a case study of Midwest Urban County,[1] examines the responses of criminal justice policymakers to changing conditions resulting from a federal suit focusing on jail overcrowding and related conditions.

Under normal circumstances the criminal justice system is relatively unconstrained, with the various actors pursuing their own priorities. Each decision maker can pursue particularized goals, irrespective of the policies and actions of other key officials. Essentially, decision makers in the criminal justice system have the discretion to carry out widely divergent and sometimes contradictory policies limited only by the broad confines of the law and political accountability. This state of affairs does not, typically, represent a departure from traditional purposes. Rather, it reflects a commitment to the notion that the public's interests are protected best by separation of authority, and that in the criminal justice area, it is inappropriate to centralize policymaking authority in one institution.

Despite the prospect for contradictory policies there is a thread that binds the process together and diminishes the likelihood of conflict. The common bond of the entire system is the ideology of incarceration (Byrne and Yanich, 1983). This is the widely shared conviction that incarceration is the appropriate response to criminal behavior in society. Policies differ from one subunit of the system to another, but they share a common direction toward the goal of incarceration of offenders.

The combination of the relatively unconstrained nature of decision making and the ideology of incarceration have had significant implications for the focal point of system activities—the county jail. The principal implication has been an overwhelming tendency of the process to overutilize detention facilities, particularly because the participants do not share responsibility for the costs incurred. This causes difficulty because jails have a finite number of bed spaces to offer, yet the other actors of the criminal justice system (judges, police, prosecutors) typically do not (and perhaps should not) take this into account in pursuing their own policies.

Overcrowded conditions and dilapidated physical structures have drawn attention to local jails since at least the mid-1960s (Matlick and Aikman, 1969). Little has been done to alleviate these conditions, and it appears that left to their own devices, the principal policymakers of local criminal justice would tolerate such conditions indefinitely (Reixach and Weimer, 1982). The inaction of local officials concerning jail problems has sparked intervention by the federal courts. Increasingly in recent years the federal courts have entertained equity suits by prisoners seeking redress for the conditions of county jails and have granted injunctive relief (McCoy, 1982; Ostrowski, 1983). Federal judges are ordering local officials to improve conditions or face the prospect of contempt of court charges or the imposition of a "federal master" to take over administration of the detention facilities.[2] What this means is that constraints are being imposed from outside the local criminal justice system that are forcing reassessment of the policies that lead to jail overcrowding. The experience of Midwest Urban County provides insight into the impact of federal court intervention in local criminal justice.

Both before and after court intervention, the criminal justice system of Midwest Urban County was characterized by various agencies pursuing different and sometimes conflicting goals, typically operating with considerable autonomy.

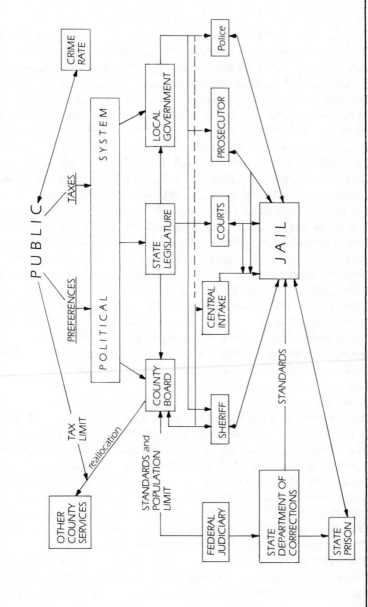

Figure 7.1   Jail Policy Network *Before* Federal Court Intervention

SYSTEM WITHOUT CONSTRAINT

Figure 7.1 characterizes the jail policy network of Midwest Urban County before federal court intervention. One characteristic of the policy network is that the decision makers in the system are relatively unconstrained. Without constraint, the police could easily respond to public calls to clean up a particular neighborhood by making a sweep and arresting all suspected prostitutes. This would alleviate political pressure on the police and funnel an additional population into the jail. Similarly, the courts could pursue a politically safe bail policy that would result in the incarceration of many individuals because of inability to arrange even a moderate bond. If a particular judge wished to initiate a harsh policy toward nonpayment of child-support cases, it would not be necessary for the jurist to consider the population pressures of the jail. Likewise, the prosecutor responding to an outbreak of home burglaries, and the resultant public outcry, could seek longer sentences for this offense. In the absence of external constraint, the size of the jail population generally was not perceived as a problem by these decision makers.

One important consideration is that the widely shared incarceration ideology of criminal justice decision makers appears strongly to be supported by the public. Organized public groups have pressed for tougher sentences for convicted offenders of specific categories of crime such as drunk drivers, nonpayers of child support, prostitutes, and so on.

The county governing board was only tangentially concerned with the overuse of jail facilities in the unconstrained situation. Although it is true that the board ultimately appropriated the funds to pay the bills, the relative proportion of county budgets devoted to jails did not need to increase greatly, even if the inmate population grew. In fact, unit cost per inmate would be reduced by overcrowded conditions as most of the costs of a jail are "fixed." It does not cost a great deal to provide an additional 40 or 50 mattresses for prisoners to sleep on the floor of cells that are used at twice their rated capacity.

In the unconstrained situation, the overcrowded jail was seen as a solution rather than a problem. System actors could pursue their own priorities and increase the jail population at little or no real cost to their agencies. In such a situation overuse of the jail is easy to understand.

SYSTEM UNDER CONSTRAINT

A proposed consent decree entered into in 1980 and renewed in 1982 by the county board and the federal district court placed specific constraints on use of the jail.

Figure 7.2 illustrates the jail policy network after federal court intervention. It is clear that the policy network described in Figure 7.2 is substantially more complicated than was the case prior to federal judicial involvement. Federal intervention had the effect of increasing the constraints on local criminal justice operations and on decision makers. Although some increase in constraints might have occurred regardless of federal intervention, both the immediacy and the extent of such developments was magnified by that intervention. Although neither figure represents a closed system, the explicit addition of the federal court and subsequently the state department of corrections expanded the boundary of the system. As the system becomes more open it is "more amenable to the contemplation of social change" (Munro, 1971: 631).

The first and most widespread effect of the federal lawsuit was a change in the role and significance of the jail in shaping local criminal justice policy. Before intervention the jail was employed as a solution for problems by local criminal justice decision makers. After the federal lawsuit, the jail itself has become the most pressing problem for local criminal justice policymakers and the solution to the problem places constraints on the choices available to those policymakers.

One of the most significant actions of the federal judge was to involve the State Department of Corrections as an active partner in dealing with problems of the jail. The state agency had developed standards relating to structural conditions, service levels, and capacity. Prior to the lawsuit these standards were routinely ignored by Midwest Urban County. As part of the compliance process with space standards the consent decree limited the population of the jail to 252 residents. This introduced a major constraint for the local criminal justice system, as prior to the lawsuit the jail frequently housed 450-500 prisoners. Further, the state standards forced the county to provide certain additional services for inmates. Enforcement of the state standards required Midwest Urban County to employ a substantially larger professional staff, including eight social workers, a part-time psychiatrist and health-care personnel. These changes, obviously, increased the cost of operating the jail.

An important and controversial aspect of the consent decree has been the expansion of the power of the county sheriff. Under the

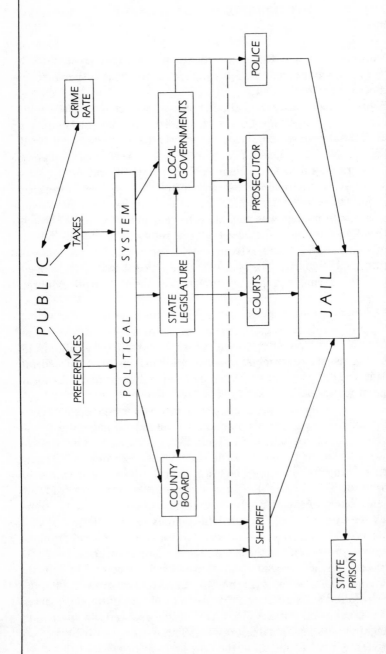

Figure 7.2   Jail Policy Network *After* Federal Court Intervention

federal order, the sheriff specifically has been granted release power over certain categories of sentenced and unsentenced inmates. This release power has engendered strong opposition from certain local judges who view it as infringement on judicial prerogatives (Price et al., 1983).

Another provision of the federal court order required the county to establish a central intake program designed to reduce overcrowding of the jail. The program represents a pretrial services approach that stresses early screening of inmates for bail recommendations and eligibility for prosecutorial diversion. The objective is to assure that all eligible inmates are released prior to trial. In practice, however, the central intake program can only recommend bail and diversion. Ultimately it is the local judges and prosecutor who decide.

Local law enforcement policies have likewise been affected by the federal court intervention. Because of space limitations at the jail, local police organizations now routinely issue appearance tickets rather than taking suspects of nonserious crimes into custody. This has severely limited the ability to respond to pressures to reduce prostitution in or near the downtown business districts. The consent decree has been attacked by police because they contend that criminals are freed "before the officers can finish filling out the incident report."

Finally, and probably most importantly, the lawsuit by prisoners has had an enormous impact on the spending priorities of the Board of Commissioners of Midwest Urban County. Specifically, the security and staffing levels at the jail are now established by the federal consent decree rather than prior practices. The effect has been to increase the security budget of the jail from $1,928,880 in 1979 to $6,449,495 in 1983. This increase of roughly 232 percent has altered the shape of the rest of the county budget, as approximately 5 million dollars have had to be reallocated from other county functions. It should be noted that this increased jail expenditures has occurred during a deep national recession.

Thus one of the major policy implications of the increased jail expenditures necessitated by the federal court order has been to bring the entire range of county service into the jail policy network. The county has had to reallocate a large amount of money from other services. The extent of this reallocation is examined below. It is important to recognize this new element in the policy network. In the past, other county services were only tangentially related to the jail policy, even though they were funded from the same source. Under the federal court consent decree it is painfully obvious to the county that each dollar increase for jail funding requires a reduction in other functions of the county.

The new relationship between the jail and other services is compounded by the resistance of the public to greater tax burdens. Recently, county taxpayers overwhelmingly rejected a millage increase to pay for the construction of a new jail to alleviate jail overcrowding.

In addition to the factors stemming from the federal suit, overcrowded conditions at the state penal institutions have created a backlog of prisoners awaiting transfer. This again has increased the stress at the county jail because the policymakers are relatively powerless to change the overcrowding problems at state prisons but must deal with the further impact of jail overcrowding as a consequence.

CHARACTERISTICS OF
JAIL POPULATION

Some implications of the population limitation order can be illustrated by an examination of Midwest Urban County Jail approximately four years after the federal court intervention. Booking data for 1982 indicated that 8585 persons had entered the county jail and remained for periods of time varying from a few minutes to one year. This number represented approximately 2 percent of the total county population of 450,000 (1980). The data show that 87.5 percent were male, 12.5 percent female; 64.7 percent were single, 19.9 percent married, and 12.2 percent divorced. Of those booked, 48.5 percent were Black (Blacks represent 17.5 percent of the county population) and 49.9 percent were White (80.5 percent of the county population). Some 7446 of these records could be classified by booking offense (by first charge listed). Of those so classified, 41 percent were charged with "civil offenses" (including traffic violations and contempt of court charges), 38 percent were charged with crimes considered "nonviolent," and 21 percent with crimes considered "violent."[3]

It should be noted that the booking record data do not reflect the composition of the jail population, as the proportion of civil detainees is exaggerated. This was confirmed by a case-by-case examination of the resident population based on a weekly census taken in October 1982. Data from this census are presented in Table 7.1. The actual proportion of resident inmates who were civil detainees was 7.3 percent, rather than the 49 percent reflected in the booking figures. The vast majority of those booked for minor nonviolent and civil infrac-

TABLE 7.1 **Jail Population**

Charges	Circuit Court			District Court #1 (Suburban)			District Court #2 (City)			Total Inmates			
	Sent.	Unsent.	Total	Sent.	Unsent.	Total	Sent.	Unsent.	Total	Sent.	Unsent.	Total	Percentage
Violent	6	57	63	10	4	14	0	18	18	16	79	95	24.7
Nonviolent	45	85	130	33	21	54	8	23	31	86	129	215	55.8
Civil	25	3	28	0	0	0	0	0	0	25	3	28	7.3
Total	76	145	211	43	25	68	8	41	49	127	211	338	
Not assigned to judge												33	8.6
Detainees												14	3.6
Total inmates												385	
(Percentage of total)	19.7	37.7	57.4	11.2	6.5	17.7	2.1	10.6	12.7	32.9	54.8		100.0

Sent. = sentenced; Unsent. = unsentenced.
NOTE: Data in this table are drawn from enumeration of persons incarcerated in urban county jail on Tuesday, October 26, 1982. For individuals with multiple convictions or charges, classification was based on a sentence taking precedence over a pretrial confinement, and a more serious charge taking precedence over a less serious charge.

tions are released within a very short period of time and never become "residents."

The federal court required that the population be limited to 252 inmates in the jail previously housing 450 to 500. We found that the limit was routinely exceeded; for example, the jail population was 355 on April 1, 1981; 342 on March 1, 1982; and 385 on October 26, 1982. Prospects of holding the population within the limit would seem to lie in the possibility of reducing the number of nonviolent and civil detainees, as release of those charged with violent crimes would present a greater danger to society. The data indicate that 45 percent of those charged with nonviolent or civil crimes would have to be released or diverted to other lower security institutions in order to meet the limit of 252. Because civil and nonviolent classifications represent 79 percent of those booked and 63 percent of the inmates actually in residence when the data in Table 7.1 were compiled, the system appears to be responding to a limited degree in the appropriate direction. However, further disaggregation of the data shows that the apparent response is explained totally by release of the civil detainees, of whom only one in seven was held overnight or longer. This reduction can be explained almost entirely by the release power granted to the sheriff by the federal judge because those having the highest priority for release are civil detainees. Considering only those detained for criminal offenses, the proportion of nonviolent offenders held overnight or longer (69 percent) was actually slightly higher than the proportion (65 percent) of nonviolent offenders among all those booked on criminal charges.

Although policies of each of the organizations in the system—police, prosecutor, and the courts— affect the composition of the jail population, the final decisions are made by the courts. The extensive literature on courts has established that differences in judicial philosophy and temperament can produce varying outcomes for individuals before the court (Brereton and Casper, 1981; Eisenstein and Jacob, 1977; Hogarth, 1971). Our findings confirmed substantial variations in judicial behavior in Midwest Urban County, both between the three courts and within each court (Price, et al., 1983). One judge (among seven) of the circuit court (felony court for this jurisdiction) was responsible for 42.8 percent of all inmates jailed for civil contempt. Most of these were detained for nonpayment of child support. The same judge accounted for 37.9 percent of all inmates detained for nonviolent crimes and was also responsible for the longest jail sentences awarded. Our data indicate that the composition of case loads was similar among judges and that differential sentencing patterns were not explained by differential assignments, but reflected different sentencing approaches.

The two lower courts are organized so that one has jurisdiction over offenses committed in the central city (District Court 2) and the other over those committed in suburban communities (District Court 1). Jail time was awarded almost four times as often by suburban judges as by city judges. The proportion of sentenced inmates attributable to the suburban court increased from 22 percent in 1981 to 32.3 percent in October of 1982. Over the same period, the proportion of sentenced inmates from city court declined from 11.1 percent to 6 percent. The variations between the 1981 and 1982 sentenced populations indicate that the reactions of the three courts to the population restriction have been quite different.

BUDGETARY EFFECTS OF COURT-MANDATED CHANGES

Budgetary effects of the court-mandated changes in the operation of the county jail became apparent almost immediately. In the short run, the increased cost of jail operation was due primarily to imposition of state service and staffing standards rather than the population limitation. Although the population limitation did inflict a substantial constraint on the ability of system participants to impose jail sentences on offenders, it had little short-term effect on the county budget. In the long run, overcrowding will require the county to remodel or replace the existing facility, which will have obvious fiscal impact. The court-mandated changes that increased the cost of operating the county jail occurred in a very difficult period for county budget managers. Midwest Urban County, like many others in the region, has been mired in an economic recession since 1979. Thus increased local revenues were not available to ease the effects of increased jail expenses. At the same time, the state and federal governments were limiting revenue sharing support. The result has been a county budget in which purchasing power fell almost 12 percent in four years. There are, therefore, two separate budgetary problems involved: the increasing cost of maintaining the county jail stemming from the court order, and at the same time an overall restriction in revenues reflecting the areawide three-year economic recession. As it was considered impossible to raise revenues sufficiently to support the increased cost of operating the jail, the County Commission made substantial changes in the departmental allocations of existing revenues.

Interdepartmental changes in budget share from 1977 to 1983 are shown in Table 7.2. The impact on two departments, the County Sheriff and Economic Development, was particularly severe. The security portion of the sheriff's budget grew from 5.7 percent to 11.2 percent of the total county budget in the year of the court order, and to 15.9 percent by 1983. Prior to 1979, security expenditures had consistently maintained a budget share in the 5 percent range. Conversely, law enforcement and community protection expenditures of the sheriff's department fell from 6.5 percent of the budget in 1979 to 1.7 percent in 1983. Community enrichment and development programs of the Economic Development Department lost about half of their budget share, as the board sought to balance overall revenues and expenditures in the face of the mandated increases in costs of operating the jail. Other county departments were not affected appreciably in terms of budget share.

Although the total budget for the sheriff's department was increased following the court decree in order to implement the mandated changes, most of the increased cost was absorbed by the department through reduced nonsecurity expenditures. The data in Table 7.3 show a 351 percent increase in security expenditures from 1977 to 1983 (173 percent after deflating by the Consumer Price Index). Nonsecurity expenditures fell 16.5 percent in the same period (-49.6 percent in lost purchasing power).

In 1980, the total number of personnel in the sheriff's department was reduced in response to budget pressures. Personnel expenditures, however, doubled from \$1,526,548 to \$3,110,749 as increased staffing of the jail was accomplished via overtime and transfer of deputies from road patrol duties. New full-time security related workers were

TABLE 7.2   Changes in Budget Share 1977-1983

	1977	*1979*	*1980*	*1981*	*1983*	*Change in Share*
Management and planning	18.5	18.5	17.7	16.1	15.7	−2.8
Administration of justice	24.3	24.6	25.4	25.0	25.9	+1.6
Law enforcement and community protection	7.1	6.5	3.7	2.0	1.7	−5.4
Human services	22.6	18.8	19.1	18.5	19.6	−3.0
Community enrichment and development	6.6	8.4	4.7	3.9	3.3	−3.3
General support	15.7	17.5	18.2	17.2	17.9	+2.2
Sheriff's security	5.2	5.7	11.2	16.2	15.9	+10.7
County general fund	100.0	100.0	100.0	100.0	100.0	

SOURCE: County Controller Data.

TABLE 7.3 Sheriff Department Budget 1977-1983

	1977	1979	1980	1981	1983	% Change
Sheriff budget (millions)	$ 3.73	5.19	6.33	7.73	8.37	124.4
Security	1.43	1.93	3.76	6.20	6.45	351.0
% Security	38.3	37.2	59.4	80.2	77.1	
Sheriff employment	133	182	160.5	192.5	196.5	+47.7
Security	59	68	68	133	155	+162.7
% Security	44.4	37.4	42.4	69.1	78.9	
Total county (millions, 1977 dollars)	$ 27.74	33.55	33.62	38.20	40.45	+45.8
Budget comparisons (millions, 1977 dollars)						
County total	27.74	27.98	24.70	25.02	24.52	−11.6
Sheriff total	3.73	4.33	4.65	5.06	5.07	+35.90
Sheriff security	1.43	1.61	2.76	4.06	3.91	+173
Sheriff nonsecurity	2.30	2.72	1.89	1.00	1.16	−49.6

SOURCE: County Controller Data.

hired starting in 1981, which has increased total employment in the department to 196.5 in 1983. The proportion involved in jail security has risen to 78.8 percent of the workers in the department, compared to 37.4 percent in 1979. The jail used 94 guards in 1983 (versus 48 in 1979) to provide the 24-hour surveillance mandated. In addition, there are eight new social workers, four new nurses, eight added administrators, and six clerk-typists to provide the required services and maintain the required records.

Thus the budgetary effects of the federal consent decree coupled with the economic recession and price inflation have reduced the enrichment and development programs of the county and substantially altered the operation of the sheriff's department. The primary role of the sheriff's department has changed from law enforcement to the operation and maintenance of the county jail. Because the results of these changes on crime rates and on the future economic development of the county may not be apparent for some time, it is doubtful that the federal court considered these effects when it ordered extensive reforms of the county jail.

INTERPRETATIONS AND CONCLUSIONS

The criminal justice system of Midwest Urban County is composed of a complex set of interrelationships among semiautonomous decision makers. Intervention of the federal court to deal with jail conditions imposed some constraints on local decision makers, as well as having a significant impact on county governance and budget. Those charged with implementing the court order (sheriff and county governing board) have had difficulty coping with the semiautonomous nature of the criminal justice policy network.

With the county jail as a focal point, the analysis provides examples of some of the effects or results of the federal court intervention into the criminal justice process in Midwest Urban County. Further, the budgetary data demonstrate a real political impact that the jail crisis had imposed on the county fiscal position. This treatment does not exhaust the consideration of the policy questions related to federal involvement with jail overcrowding. Rather, it is intended to exemplify the types of considerations that must be addressed in a policy analysis of the situation.

NOTES

1. We have chosen "Midwest Urban County" as the name of the locality that we are investigating in order to protect the identity of our sources. This precaution was thought necessary because litigation is still in progress, and some of the officials were reluctant to comment if they would be quoted by name in a national forum.

2. A federal master is an official appointed by a federal judge to oversee the administration of a local jail or prison. For example, a federal master was appointed for Lucas County, Ohio after repeated failures by the local facility to reduce overcrowding and improve conditions. This process occurred via a prisoner lawsuit and the federal master was appointed after the construction of a new jail also failed to improve conditions.

3. Crimes classified as violent included all situations in which force was threatened or used against another person. Examples are homicide, assault, rape, robbery, manslaughter, and arson. Crimes classified as nonviolent were essentially property offenses such as larceny, breaking and entering, drugs, and stolen property. Civil offenses refers to civil contempt for nonpayment of child support and traffic violations.

REFERENCES

BRERETON, D. and J. CASPER (1981-1982) "Does it pay to plead guilty? Differential sentencing and the functioning of criminal courts." *Law and Society Review* 16(1): 45.

BYRNE, J. and D. YANICH (1983) "The ideology of incarceration and the cooptation of correctional reform," in J. W. Doiq (ed.), *Criminal Corrections: Ideals and Realities.* Lexington, MA: D. C. Heath.

EISENSTEIN, J. and H. JACOB (1977) *Felony Justice.* Boston: Little, Brown.

HARRIS, M. K. and D. P. SPILLER, Jr. (1976) *After Decision: Implementation of Judicial Decrees in Correctional Settings;* Washington, DC: American Bar Association.

HOGARTH, J. (1971) *Sentencing as a Human Process.* Toronto: University of Toronto Press.

MATLICK, H. W. and A. B. AIKMAN (1969) "The cloacal region of American corrections." *The Annals of the American Academy of Political and Social Science* 381: 109.

McCOY, C. (1982) "New federalism, old remedies, and corrections policy-making." *Policy Studies Review* 2: 271.

MUNRO, J. L. (1971) "Towards a theory of criminal justice administration: a general systems approach." *Public Administration Review* 31(621): 631.

OSTROM, V. (1974) *The Intellectual Crisis in American Public Administration.* University, AL: University of Alabama Press.

OSTROWSKI, T. S. (1983) "Judicial intervention and jail reform," in J. W. Doig (ed.), *Criminal Corrections: Ideals and Realities.* Lexington, MA: D. C. Heath.

PRICE, A. C., C. WEBER, and E. PERLMAN (1983) "Judicial discretion and jail overcrowding." *Justice System Journal* 8: 222.

REIXACH, K. A. and D. WEIMER (1982) "A note on America's 'cloacal' jails." *Policy Studies Review* 2: 239.

8.

CONTEMPORARY DOCTRINES OF CIVIL DEATH

George H. Cox, Jr.
David M. Speak
Georgia Southern College

Most of the criminal justice policy developed in the United States is generated by state and local governments. Corrections policy is no exception. The governance of American prisons and jails is largely the concern of state and local governments, respectively. State prisons have come under the scrutiny of federal district courts in cases involving the civil rights and living conditions of prison inmates. Federal court activism in this area of prisoner rights promises to be one of the most significant stimuli for prison reform in this decade. However, the basis of federal court intervention is as yet fragmentary. A clarification of the basic issues involved in court-ordered prison reform is necessary if the long-term impact of that intervention is to be assessed.

The rights of persons who are imprisoned in the United States are the subject of considerable speculation. Beyond the obvious loss of the liberty of movement, what rights are forfeited at the time of incarceration? Why are these rights lost and others retained? What have the courts and administrators said about prisoner rights? How should issues like prisoners' citizenship status be evaluated? What questions should be asked about such evaluations? This analysis explores the status of the inmates in state prisons in the United States in an effort to address these questions.

WHAT RIGHTS ARE FORFEITED
AT THE TIME OF INCARCERATION?

Two distinct lines of development are present in talking about the specific loss of rights experienced by persons when they are imprisoned in the United States. The first, apparently—but not often explicitly—based on the old common-law notion of civil death, holds that upon conviction for a serious crime a natural person ceases to be a legal person in the eyes of the convicting government. In its strongest form, this doctrine means that all legal rights are withdrawn from the individual. Even under modern variants of this doctrine, a broad loss of citizenship rights is experienced at the time of incarceration. A person suffers many civil disabilities in the form of forfeited or restricted enjoyment of rights such as marriage, contracting, voting, and holding public office. More broadly under this viewpoint, a person becomes "the slave of the state" (Ruffin v. Commonwealth of Virginia, 1871) because the exclusionary provision of the Thirteenth Amendment does not forbid involuntary servitude "as a punishment for crime whereof the party shall have been duly convicted." A person may, therefore, have claims upon the government for protection from physical abuse and deprivation, but this and other protections are those offered to all persons within the United States under the Eighth Amendment ban on "cruel and unusual punishments" rather than those assured citizens as political liberties elsewhere in the Constitution and, more broadly, in the culture. In popular form, this doctrine of civil death is tied to the argument that one has forfeited one's civil rights by transgressing a major social rule. These forefeited rights are commonly reinstated after serving one's time in prison. In this first line of government, the analogy of death may not be strong enough to represent the complete loss of rights, for even dead persons have rights and can make claims on the state through wills, estates, and executors.

The second line of argument extends *some* legal protections to convicted persons, but clearly at a lower level than the rights afforded ordinary persons. Prisoners have several diverse, legally acknowledged rights, including the rights of access to counsel, to send and receive mail, and to enjoy certain minimal provisions for personal safety while incarcerated (Rudovsky et al., 1983). The most extreme statement of this second line—a general doctrine of universal citizenship—holds that citizenship is established in the United States by birth or by naturalization under the Fourteenth Amendment (Rubin, 1971). An individual may renounce citizenship or lose it by offering allegiance to another nation state, but the government may not remove citizenship. Citizenship "is not a license that expires upon misbehavior" (Trop v. Dulles, 1958). Under this viewpoint, any restrictions that are placed on the political liberties of prison inmates must be shown to be directly related to protecting the security of the institution (Procunier v. Martinez, 1974; Pell v. Procunier, 1974). Moreover, a prison sentence involves confinement with the prisoner retaining all rights of the citizen except those removed by law, either expressly or by necessary implication, such as, the right to bear arms (Coffin v. Reichard, 1944). Under this viewpoint, there are few necessary constraints of citizenship represented by correctional custody other than secure containment, and many valid citizenship rights of prisoners are now correctly being recognized (e.g., voting, in Tate v. Collins, 1980).

These two distinct trends in defining the status of convicted persons, although not antithetical, are at least in opposition to one another. For one to advance, the other must retreat. One might mistakenly characterize these two lines of development as existing in chronological succession, with the old civil death notion being replaced by a new Eighth Amendment assertion of "prisoners' rights" (Palmer, 1977), but this characterization fails to adequately encompass the present state of flux. The current situation can best be characterized as one of conceptual confusion, in which—due to compartmentalized thinking and mutually inconsistent institutional behaviors—contradictory notions exist side by side.

WHY ARE SOME RIGHTS
LOST AND OTHERS RETAINED?

Corrections administrators are often aware of the logical and legal arguments of these two extreme positions as they seek to express their own interest in such matters. Both they and some members of the federal judiciary have sometimes tried to find an official "compromise" position on the constitutional status of prisoners:

> Imprisonment by its very nature deprives the offender of some constitutional rights. It is not clear, however, which rights must be completely sacrificed and which may be retained, perhaps in modified form [Allen and Simonsen, 1981].

If the prisoner has legitimate claims upon citizenship rights and the prison administrator has legitimate prerogatives associated with proper security and confinement, then some assert that a doctrine of the "balance of interests" between the state and the individual is operative (Archambeault, 1982). Other prison administrators develop policies that lean more toward one or the other poles in the controversy rather than consciously seeking middle ground. States of the Southeast and far West tend to operate prison systems under civil death assumptions.

Those of the Northeast and upper Midwest tend more toward the citizenship perspective. Unfortunately, most states are unclear about the basis for their policies concerning prisoners' rights.

The argument developed in this chapter is that the status quo is unstable and unacceptable, and that conceptual clarification may mean making a choice between the two doctrines currently being promulgated. We contend here that the citizenship perspective has equal or even superior claims upon the common-law traditions of American political development, as does the more common civil death outlook in prison law. This is especially true when one explores the contemporary development of legal principles as a dynamic, culturally-based process that neither begins nor ends with the promulgation of statutory law. The political culture and the law continue to develop or evolve as the society explicates its values and traditions.

The analysis also examines the prevalent civil death assumptions and their citizenship alternatives in two areas of inmate life, privacy rights, and work rights. Overall, prisoners suffer a total loss of the right to privacy and the right to the fruits of their own labor when they are confined. Under the citizenship perspective, such loss is not implied in the loss of liberty of movement represented by correctional confinement. Few arguments are advanced that both privacy rights and work rights are curtailed because of security needs. More often, appeals for restriction on these rights (e.g., limited mail and token wages) are made based on externalities such as cost to the state, administrative convenience, or the rehabilitative needs of the inmate population. Most court activism that has occurred has based its recognition of inmate rights on protections from cruel and unusual punishment, rights enjoyed by all persons residing in the United States, not citizens alone. Even more to the point, these later restrictions are drawn as prohibitions on government action rather than recognition of citizenship rights. Professional and judicial appeals to such externalities may ultimately damage the case for full citizenship recognition for prisoners. This type of "reform" may weaken and not strengthen the protections afforded prison inmates because scattered and isolated "privileges" such as miniscule wages and once-a-month, directly supervised visits by "approved" persons are inferior to rights attendant to United States citizenship.

As the common law continues to develop the right to privacy and work rights, the extension of these rights to prisoners should be total and automatic. Restrictions should be piecemeal and individually justified. The current correctional systems in the states have the relationship backwards. They have reversed the principle of citizenship to exclude all rights other than those recognized or granted by the corrections department. At the heart of their penal systems is the general doctrine of civil death, alive and well in the twentieth century. It is far from demise as a legal doctrine, even though the bases for its reasoning (e.g., property and work duties to the feudal lord) are obsolete. Variants of the general doctrine instead persist as unexamined, unjustified bundles of prejudice and self-service.

WHAT HAVE COURTS AND ADMINISTRATORS DONE ABOUT INMATE RIGHTS?

There now exists a large body of case law that extends a wide variety of protections to convicted persons. Even Justice Rehnquist, writing for the Court in a case rejecting prisoners' claim to the right to organize, characterizes constitutional rights as limited rather than extinguished by incarceration:

> The fact of confinement and the needs of the penal institution impose limitations on constitutional rights, including those derived from the First Amendment, which are implicit in incarceration. . . . Perhaps the most obvious of the First Amendment rights that are necessarily curtailed by confinement are those associational rights that the First Amendment protects outside of prison walls [Jones v. North Carolina Prisoners' Labor Union, Inc., 1977].

Chief Justice Burger, concurring in the same case, concludes:

> This recognition (that federal courts are not equipped to second guess state legislators and administrators in this sensitive area), of course, does not imply that the prisoner is stripped of all constitutional protection as he passes through the prison's gates. Indeed, this Court has made clear on numerous occasions that the Constitution and other federal laws protect certain basic rights of inmates [Jones v. North Carolina Prisoners' Labor Union, Inc., 1977].

These statements come from the two members of the current Court whose philosophies are least sympathetic to prisoners' rights. They indicate, in contradistinction to civil death, the well-established position of specific, narrow rights claims that prisoners enjoy. These case law protections reinforce and are reinforced by the commensurate protections in constitution and statute.

In terms of establishing and reporting narrow civil disabilities and protections, existing legal analysis may be adequate. It is in terms of understanding the broad presumption of rights lost at the time of incarceration that contemporary analysis suffers. Privacy rights and work rights affect the very heart of a prisoner's daily life. An examination of current practice in these areas indicates the simultaneous practice and denial of the doctrine of civil death.

Privacy in Prison

Individuals confined in state prisons have few opportunities to experience confidentiality in their personal lives or exercise independence in making personal decisions. Both the institutional rules and the general conditions of today's prisons combine to traumatize and "prisonize" men and women who are confined (Allen and Simonsen, 1981). Life in an American prison may violate one's privacy rights so thoroughly that the inmate may be said to be under continuous psychic assault.

Prisoners' person and property are subjected to frequent searches in correctional institutions. Efforts to find weapons and contraband involve routine "shakedowns" of living space (Fox, 1983), and careful body searches are conducted when prisoners have been in contact with the outside world or people from outside the prison (Rudovsky et al., 1983). Many articles of personal property are not allowed into the living areas of a prison—such as stamps, cash, and valuable wrist watches—because such items are said to become the objects of theft and trade, leading to conflict within the inmate population. Valuable personal property and money are stored for prisoners until their release, and some pains are taken to assure the prisoner that his or her property is accounted for during confinement (American Correctional Association, 1966).

The amount of property (and space, for that matter) available to each prisoner is, of course, quite limited. Institutional rules commonly prohibit the wearing of personal clothing; uniforms are issued to all inmates. Bed linen is standard issue, as well. Personal articles like magazines and books, a radio, and family photographs, letters, and food stuffs from home may be restricted, especially when crowded dormitory or cell conditions make clutter a problem and lockers difficult logistically.

Personal appearance is also regulated. Individuals are required to adhere to a haircut code in many prisons, and facial hair may be prohibited. Moreover, consistent efforts are made to ensure uniform appearances of the confined law offenders.

Correspondence and visitation with the inmate are controlled in some important respects. Family members and approved friends may correspond with and visit a prisoner under the close supervision of security personnel at the correctional institution. Incoming mail is opened and screened, and the amount of mail is restricted to an amount that can be censored (Allen and Simonsen, 1981). Visitor lists must be approved, and the number and frequency of visits by an approved person are constrained in most states.

Daily routines consist of assignments to various tasks made by the prison staff. Inmates rarely choose where they will sleep or work or spend their off-hours.

The combined effects of restriction on property, appearance, communications, and choice, and the frequent intrusion of prison staff into these areas represent a serious challenge to one's self-image and self-esteem. Some rules of prison life are calculated to reduce the range of personal choice and expression (e.g., the restrictions on appearance); others are perhaps the result of crowded group living situations and overextended staff (e.g., limits of possessions and number of pieces of mail). Yet the assault on the privacy of the individual inmate is overwhelming. There appear to be broad presumptions of the loss of privacy rights that attend confinement in American state prisons.

Room searches are permitted by the federal courts as long as the inmate is officially advised of items seized and as long as personal property is not unnecessarily destroyed (Wolfish v. Levi, 1978; Steinberg v. Taylor, 1980; Clifton v. Robinson, 1980; Brown v. Hilton, 1980). Neither may property be seized during cell or dormitory searches if the items are not prohibited as contraband (O'Connor v. Keller, 1981). "Significant governmental interests" (Bell v. Wolfish, 1979) are involved in the efforts to control weapons and contraband in prisons, such as when books are sent to inmates by persons other than the publisher. There are, moreover, rationales that purport to justify room searches in terms of the security and good order of the correctional institution.

Searches of one's person are allowed as well, as long as they are conducted "in a reasonable manner" (Bell v. Wolfish, 1979). Under Bell, an inmate enjoys the right to be spared derogatory remarks during strip searches. Furthermore, a prisoner is not required to submit to such a search in the presence of a correctional officer of the opposite sex (Rudovsky et al., 1983). It is also necessary to establish the fact that outside contact has taken place in order to justify a strip (visual body cavity) search (Bono v. Saxbe, 1980; Ruiz v. Estelle, 1980). Body searches, like room searches, may be reasoned to be essential to the proper operation of the prison.

National corrections standards call for the limitation of searches and constraint in the removal of personal property. Specifically, they have called for "avoiding undue or unnecessary force, embarrassment, or indignity to the individual" and "conducting searches no more frequently than reasonably necessary to control contraband in the institution or to recover missing or stolen property" (National Advisory Commission on Criminal Justice Standards and Goals, 1973). This general sentiment supporting some privacy rights in the area of the right of inmates to be secure "in their persons, houses, papers, and effects, against unreasonable searches and seizures" is not now a recognized Fourth Amendment protection. Critics have noted that the courts instead tend to side with corrections officials who "insist that the right to privacy ceases to exist on entry into the penal institution" (Rudovsky et al., 1983).

A pattern of courts failing to recognize the privacy rights of prisoners exists to a lesser extent in the areas of personal appearance, mail and visitation, and freedom of choice. However, in each of these areas, the support that has developed for inmate rights appeals to externalities rather than the benefits of citizenship per se. Rights may exist but not on a foundation of rights-holding citizenship.

Prison officials have argued that health and security (personal identification) interests of the institution justify the requirement that all prisoners conform to a short hairstyle. In some instances, the courts have allowed the institutionalized law offenders to claim a preincarceration religious conviction requiring that a man wear a beard (Maguire v. Wilkinson, 1975). This appeal to First Amendment protections would extend to noncitizens as well as citizens because it constrains government actions that infringe upon religious exercise. Again, the basis of the protection is, therefore, external to the issue of citizenship rights. Neither does the protection extend to the broad majority of prison inmates who would not have been likely to have established a recognized religious practice affecting appearance before confinement.

Mail and visitation are controlled in terms of the persons with whom one can correspond and visit, and in terms of the conditions under which letters or visits are supervised. Rationales for each of these regulations are based on the "clear and present danger" criterion that the courts have recognized in the unrestricted flow of communication between the prisoner and other people.

Correspondence and visitation between inmates are usually not allowed. Friends or "jailhouse lawyers" at different institutions may not establish contact (Allen and Simonsen, 1981). The prison may maintain lists of approved correspondents for each inmate, and mail can be stopped for gross rule violations (Bronstein, 1980). The content of letters can be censored only if it jeopardizes the security or mission of the institution, and regulations must recognize this narrow criterion for censorship (Procunier v. Martinez, 1974). Correspondence to and from the courts is protected (Wolff v. McDonnell, 1974), but the right of attorneys and their inmate clients to correspond is subject to the examination and possible censorship of the letters if the inmate discusses "restricted matters" (Sostre v. McGinnis, 1972).

Visitation "privileges" are prescribed in virtually the same manner. The persons with whom an inmate may visit must be approved, and the list rarely includes persons other than one's attorney of record and family members. Visiting hours are restricted, and no privacy is offered husbands and wives except in those few jurisdictions in which "conjugal visits" are permitted (Fox, 1983). The courts have set very few standards that would regulate prison visitation practice. This lack of involvement may be justified in the minds of some by the observation that visitation rules constrain the manner but not the content of communications (Burke v. Levi, 1975). This would tend to place such claims under the Pell standard of reasonable restrictions concerning the status of inmates instead of the Martinez standard of civil rights protections (Calhoun, 1980).

Privacy in one's possessions, person, appearance, mail and visitation are not totally absent in the prison policies of the American states. Actual practice certainly varies by state and between prisons within a state because of the wide discretion allowed administrators. Maintaining the security of the correctional institution apparently gives the person in charge of that facility broad powers to intrude into private physical and psychological space and into communications as well. It would theoretically be possible to make such intrusion complete with the exception of correspondence with the courts, but such a totally regulated life would likely destroy the morale of the inmate population and is rare outside of maximum security facilities. Some exercise of independent judgment and some expression of individual personality results in a better adjusted, more productive prison resident (Fox, 1983). Yet local prison administrators have few coherent models of prisoner privacy rights to guide them. Various external criteria are cited for particular "rights" ranging from the rights of outside correspondents to the best rehabilitative interests of the inmate. There is certainly no effective doctrine supporting privacy rights for prisoners. Neither is there a broadly based rationale justifying the death of such rights when an individual is confined—none, that is, but the implicit doctrine of civil death.

Prison Work Practices

Prison inmates are commonly forced to work for little or no compensation. Their work duties include a wide variety of institutional maintenance, prison system support, and government agency support tasks. Compensation, when provided, is again justified with appeals to externalities such as inmate morale, inmate financial solvency when exiting prison, or the economics of prison system operations. Little support by the courts has been given to the claim of inherent work rights of prisoners (Clark and Parker, 1975).

There are four types of prison labor practice in the United States that in their requirements exceed the minimal personal maintenance duties of the confined person. Every person living in a constricted group setting from the soldier to the outdoors camper can be expected to keep his or her quarters straightened and clean. However, in addition to these personal or dormitory duties, larger institutional or system-wide duties are commonly assigned to work crews made up of prisoners and supervised by corrections staff. Such assignments are neither voluntary nor are most salaried.

The maintenance of the institution is often said to require labor-intensive projects. The renovation of old buildings, construction of recreation facilities, or the repair of shop, classroom, or farm buildings might be accomplished by inmate work crews. Skilled prisoners may install or repair plumbing and electrical wiring, operate heavy machinery, or simply provide manual labor in such endeavors. Skilled inmates are often in such demand that they function very much like staff members. In fact, they may serve in the place of a maintenance employee. This may distort the true human resource needs of correctional institutions, a fact that becomes painfully obvious when the skilled inmate leaves or wants to be transferred.

The second area of prison work is related to the first. Skilled inmate workers may be in demand at other institutions. Rather than compete for these individuals, prison systems sometimes organize mobile work crews made up of inmate specialists. Construction crews, for example, might work at several prisons during the course of a year's work, and they might perform tasks at halfway houses, county institutions, and administrative offices of the agency as well. When the need for inmate specialists is long-term, as in the case of county institutions that need heavy equipment operators for road repair on a continuing basis, the state may assign persons to the county. Typically, the state will pay for some of the costs of feeding and housing this state inmate when such an arrangement is made.

A third area of prison work supports the entire system rather than a specific institution or governmental task at a single institution. This group of tasks typically includes the production of the uniforms, bedding, and furniture used in prisons throughout the state. Similarly, the food needed throughout the prison system may be grown on large farms. In these "jobs," many unskilled prisoners may be employed as well as persons with manufacturing or agricultural backgrounds. The manufacturing of goods used in the prison system may be conducted by Correctional Industries, Inc., a public corporation chartered in many states to produce items needed in state agencies, such as school desks and license tags as well as prison uniforms and bedding. Inmate employees of Correctional Industries, Inc. are the most likely class of workers discussed so far to be paid for their work. Yet the wage rate is much lower than that paid civilian workers—salaries range from $.04 to $.19 per hour in Delaware and from $.18 to $1.40 in Illinois. Several states pay nothing for such work, such as Arkansas, Florida, Georgia, and Texas (Criminal Justice Institute, 1983).

Finally, 20 states permit private industries to operate plants inside of their prisons. A small but potentially growing number of prison inmates work for these industries, and their federal minimum wage salaries provide revenue for operating the prison through "fees for services," court ordered restitution to victims, and family support, as well as building the individual's savings account (Schaller, 1982).

The vast majority of all inmates who are incarcerated in the United States work at either local maintenance or system maintenance jobs. For example, only ten percent of all state inmates work in Correctional Industries in the United States, and one-fourth of those work in states that pay no wage for Correctional Industries work. The situation is only marginally better in the federal prison system: one-fourth of the inmates work in Correctional Industries, and the other three-fourths are part of the general labor force of the prisons (Criminal Justice Institute, 1983). Private industry jobs that pay more than the typical $.25 to $.85 paid per hour by Correctional Industries are considerably more rare. There are likely only several hundred such jobs in the entire

United States. The pervasive pattern for prison work in the country is involuntary, unpaid penal servitude.

States that pay their inmates nothing argue that the Constitution explicitly permits penal servitude when, in the Thirteenth Amendment, it provides that "Neither slavery nor involuntary servitude, except as a punishment for crime whereof the party shall have been duly convicted, shall exist within the United States, or any place subject to their jurisdiction." Prisoners are considered "slaves of the state" (Ruffin v. Commonwealth of Virginia, 1871) in these states, a class of persons who do not own the fruits of their own labors. Of the 15 states that have traditionally paid inmates nothing for their labors, 7 were slave-holding states when that practice was permitted under the Constitution.

A large number of states pay inmates some small wage for their labors, especially if the inmate is "employed" by Correctional Industries, Inc. in that state. Normal working conditions are stated to benefit the prisoner by providing him or her with skills training, instilling good work habits for later employment, giving the person some discretion over the money honestly earned through employment, and providing for the prisoner and his or her family's material needs in the short- and long-runs. This situation may be contrasted with the frequent observation that prisoners have no financial resources when they enter prison and therefore rely on the correctional agency or outside friends for tobacco, postage stamps, and other small luxuries of life. They have no resources when they leave except for a suit of clothes, a bus ticket, and a small amount of money (perhaps $25) and their families are often on welfare as a result of the loss of a breadwinner.

The tiny minority of prison inmates in the United States who earn meager wages more like those of lower-income free world workers benefit themselves and the system in ways that exceed those noted above. These "wealthier" inmates—such as those employed by private firms operating prison plants—can pay for their "room and board," pay fines and court-ordered restitution, contribute to their family's support, and thereby reduce the cost of incarceration to the state. The institution additionally benefits from a more stabilized institutional environment organized around the "work ethic": there is less idle time and inmate dissatisfaction. The prison also gets to develop collegial relationships with socially valued private enterprises (Sexton, 1982).

Work may be healthy, publicly beneficial, and in the best interests of all concerned. Indeed, the same has been said of forced labor gangs down through the history of corrections (Fox, 1983). Yet these appeals are to externalities; the right to work voluntarily and receive benefits from the fruits of one's labor are work rights. Few efforts to establish fundamental work rights of prisoners have been attempted, and those that have been tried have failed (Clark and Parker, 1975). The courts have declared that prison inmates may not organize in the work place and bargain collectively (Jones v. North Carolina Prisoners' Labor Union, 1977). They are not public employees either, so they cannot benefit from civil services protections (Salah v. Commonwealth of Pennsylvania, 1978).

There is some evidence to suggest that corrections professionals want to reform employment practices in the state prisons of the United States:

> There have been some recent suggestions that the entire system be changed. The proposal has been made that residents or inmates of prisons and correctional institutions be paid the legal minimum wage and then be charged board, room, and other maintenance. The argument is that they are citizens of the United States and should be covered by its laws [Fox, 1983: 90].

> Pay for inmates presently incarcerated is too low to be regarded as wages. Rates of pay must be increased to at least the minimum wage on the outside for similar labor [Allen and Simonsen, 1981: 67; reference to the Wickersham Commission, Lyndon Johnson's Task Force on Corrections].

Yet these ideals are not realized in today's state prison systems.

Most of the states—perhaps all of them—practice penal servitude. Some would likely admit it openly and claim that the Thirteenth Amendment protects that practice. Others would profess "moderate" postures on work rights and would justify some token wage based on various noble externalities. Still others would deny that they engage in forced labor without compensation, but the level of wages, protections in the workplace, and other conditions of the workplace suggest that full citizenship is not assumed in the case of inmate laborers. In a real sense, all three categories of states are civil death states. They simply frame their practices in different terms. When it comes to the basic facts of prison life, the broad loss of citizenship rights at the time of incarceration still occurs.

HOW SHOULD CITIZENSHIP STATUS
BE EVALUATED?

The doctrine of civil death is alive and well, though not in uncontested control of the field of relevant law. The implicit assumptions that accompany a prisoner into a state correctional institution suggest a broad loss of citizenship rights. The right to privacy and work rights are but two categories of civic benefits that have not been extended to prisoners as a class of citizens. The "prisoners' rights" that do exist are established through appeals to externalities. Little progress has been made or will likely be made in understanding the legal status of prisoners until the question of their citizenship status is addressed.

Why change things? What justifications exist for moving from the status quo with its inconsistencies between the civil death and citizenship traditions toward a clear statement of those protections that are maintained and those that of necessity must be removed? In particular, why abandon civil death in favor of the citizenship model? Such a move is supported by three sets of reasons: one legal, one administrative, and one philosophical.

Law. First, in legal terms, a large body of constitutional, statutory, and case law contradicts the basic stance of the civil death doctrine. At three separate points in the Constitution, the framers explicitly rejected the full notion of civil death, whether legislatively or judicially assigned. In addition, the Eighth Amendment prohibition of "cruel and unusual punishments" offers clear evidence that the founders were self-consciously opposed to the old European doctrine that denies all civil rights to convicted felons. The authors of the Constitution of the United States expressly forbade some of the civil death practices of their forebearers. For example, "corruption of blood" is not allowed in treason convictions, nor are "bills or attainder" stripping convicted persons of their civil rights allowed in cases of traitors condemned to death (article 3, section three, paragraph two and article 1, sections nine and ten, respectively, United States Constitution of 1787). Madison's notes on the Federal Convention reveal no controversy in accepting these clauses (James Madison's Notes on the Federal Convention, 1787). Dealing with the most serious crime against a nation, treason, the framers explicitly pare off parts of the civil death notion, loss of property and inheritance rights. This concern for proper punishment is, of course, extended in the Eighth Amendment in its prohibition of "cruel and unusual punishments." Convicted felons retained rights; they did not undergo a total demise of status when incarcerated.

The case against civil death in statutory law is as strong as the constitutional one. Even a casual survey of state criminal statutes reveals a trend away from both the explicit language of civil death and the implications of that doctrine. By 1970, only seven states retained explicit civil death statutes. Even in states where it was explicitly retained, the vigor of civil death is vitiated by the routinized practice of reinstating rights following prison terms. In sentencing, states have moved from confinement "at hard labor" to simple confinement, and even beyond simple confinement—as in work release and education release programs in which prisoners are free to join the regular work force during the day. These kinds of statutory provisions in the state codes strongly suggest that the doctrine of civil death has steadily eroded in the eyes of legislatures throughout the United States.

There now also exists a large body of case law that extends a wide variety of protections to convicted persons. Inmates of correctional institutions have rights to easy correspondence with their attorneys and the courts, they enjoy protections from physical abuse and grossly substandard living conditions, and they may vote and exercise other citizenship prerogatives under some circumstances. In contradistinction to a general doctrine of civil death, there is increasingly a well-established repertoire of narrow, specific rights for prisoners to en-

These case law protections reinforce the constitutional and statutory standards that have also sought to contradict civil death assumptions.

Moreover, there are compelling reasons for constitutional provisions like the Eighth Amendment not to bear the burden of all corrections reform policy. In the absence of a clear notion of citizenship, judges are required to use "cruel and unusual punishment" to ground their standard setting. Does it make sense to say confinement in a five-by-ten foot cell is cruel and unusual but confinement in a six-by-ten foot cell is not? To allow or encourage such manipulation of the language is a disservice to all citizens and to the legal system itself.

Administration. Second, there are strong administrative reasons for choosing the citizenship model of prisoners' rights over the status quo, the hodgepodge of citizenship rights decisions amid profound (contradictory) civil death assumptions. The first of these concerns the interaction of prison officials, state legislators, and judicial officials (both state and federal). As long as no clear definition of the status of convicted persons exists, each set of policymakers whose actions impact the corrections system must second-guess the others. Prison officials must mediate the conflicting demands of, on the one hand, legislators who seek to keep politically unpopular prison budgets as low as possible and, on the other, judges who impose upon prisons minimum standards of services based on externalities such as the Eighth Amendent rights of persons in prison. Even when well-intentioned, such mediation activity rarely satisfies all parties. Federal judges feel compelled to assert administrative control over state prisons in the face of what seem of them unresponsive policies and practices. Such activity, unavoidable when no clear conception of the status of prisoners exists, distorts the judicial role, and is corrosive to the system of federalism.

The second administrative reason for favoring the citizenship model concerns the activities of corrections officials themselves. It is impossible to achieve rational organizational behavior, much less define organizational goals and objectives, when no formal agreement exists relative to the legal status of the clientele. Can prison officials realistically be expected to formulate appropriate corrections policies when many if not most of the major restrictions on their actions are couched in terms that relate only indirectly to the individuals involved? When the warden at Soledad formulates prison mail policies, should the primary consideration be the First Amendment rights of the inmates' outside correspondents? The Supreme Court, in *Procunier v. Martinez* (1974), seems to suggest so. How much more rational it would be to develop prison policy based on the status and treatment of the prisoners themselves. The current conceptual confusion precludes this possibility; the civil death model extinguishes the existence of prisoners as persons. The only choice that allows for administrative planning is the citizenship model.

Philosophy. The final argument in favor of the citizenship model over that of civil death is a philosophical one. Liberty has long been one of the primary guiding principles of the republic. Except perhaps for the attachment to property rights, no other value enjoys such exalted status in the collective reckoning. Yet it is clear that, even if the society were willing to turn the clock back to accept civil death in its full panoply, to do so would be to sacrifice liberty for nothing of comparative value. To formulate corrections policy, as the states now do, on the basis of ad hoc, external exceptions to civil death will certainly have a tendency toward maximum restriction rather than maximum freedom. Such a practice seeks minimally acceptable levels of freedom in the context of restraint. On the other hand, to accept the citizenship model will have the reverse tendency. To acknowledge full citizenship rights for persons convicted of serious crimes, limited only by justifiable exceptions related to confinement, would favor maximum liberty yet still allow for justifiable countervailing considerations. In the absence of explicit, particular justifications of restraint, the nation of Paine and Jefferson ought to choose freedom.

CASES

BELL v. WOLFISH (1979) 441 U.S. 520
BONO v. SAXBE (1980) 620 F 2d 609 7th Cir.
BROWN v. HILTON (1980) 492 F. Supp. 771 D. NJ.
BURKE v. LEVI (1975) 391 F. Suppl 186 (E.D. Va) vacated, 530 F 2d. 967 (4th Cir. 1975)
CLIFTON v. ROBINSON (1980) 500 F. Supp. 30 E.D.Pa.
COFFIN v. REICHARD (1944) 143 F 2nd 443
MAGUIRE v. WILKINSON (1975) 405 F. Supp. 637 (D.Conn.)
JONES v. NORTH CAROLINA PRISONER'S LABOR UNION, INC. (1977) 443 U.S. 119
O'CONNOR v. KELLER (1981) 510 F. Supp. 1359 D.Md.
PELL v. PROCUNIER (1974) 417 U.S. 817
PROCUNIER v. MARTINEZ (1974) 416 U.S. 396
RUFFIN v. COMMONWEALTH OF VIRGINIA (1871) 62 Va. 790
SALAH v. COMMONWEALTH OF PENNSYLVANIA (1978) 24 Cr.L. 2249 (Penn. Commonwealth Ct.)
STEINBERG v. TAYLOR (1980) 500 F. Supp. 477 D. Conn.
TATE v. COLLINS (1980) 28 Cr.L. 2013 W.D.Tenn.
TROP v. DULLES (1958) 356 U.S. 86
WOLFF v. MCDONNELL (1974) 418 U.S. 539
WOLFISH v. LEVI (1978) 573 F 2nd 118

REFERENCES

ALLEN, H. E. and C. E. SIMONSEN (1981) Corrections in America. New York: Macmillan.
American Correctional Association (1966) Manual of Correctional Standards. Washington, DC: Author.
ARCHAMBEAULT, W. G. and B. J. ARCHAMBEAULT (1982) Correctional Supervisory Management. Englewood Cliffs, NJ: Prentice-Hall.
BRONSTEIN, A. J. (1980) "Offender rights litigation: historical and future developments," pp. 5-28 in I. P. Robbins (ed.), Prisoners' Rights Sourcebook. New York: Clark Boardman.
CALHOUN, E. (1980) "The First Amendment rights of prisoners," pp. 43-65 in I. P. Robbins (ed.), Prisoners' Rights Sourcebook. New York: Clark Boardman.
CLARK, L. D. and G. M. PARKER (1975) "The labor law problems of the prisoner." Rutgers Law Review 28(4): 840-860.
CORWIN, E. S. (1955) The "Higher Law" Background of American Constitutional Law. Ithaca, NY: Cornell University Press.
Criminal Justice Institute (1983) Corrections Yearbook. South Salem, NJ: Author.
FOX, V. (1983) Correctional Institutions. Englewood Cliffs, NJ: Prentice-Hall.
MADISON, J. (1958) "Notes on the Federal Convention," in W.U. Solberg (ed.), The Federal Convention and the Formation of the Union of the American States. Indianapolis: Bobbs-Merrill.
National Advisory Commission on Criminal Justice Standards and Goals (1973) Corrections. Washington, DC: U.S. Department of Justice.

PALMER, J. W. (1977) Constitutional Rights of Prisoners. Cincinnati: Anderson.

RUBIN, S. (1971) "The man with a record." Federal Probation Quarterly 35(3): 3-7.

RUDOVSKY, D., A. J. BRONSTEIN, and E. L. KOREN (1983) The Rights of Prisoners. New York: Bantam.

SAVAGE, R. L. (1982) "Patterns of multilinear evolution in the American states," pp. 25-28 in J. Kincaid (ed.), Political Culture, Public Policy and the American States. Philadelphia: Institute for the Study of Human Issues.

SCHALLER, J. (1982) "Work and imprisonment: an overview of the changing role of prison labor in American prisons." The Prison Journal 62: 3-12.

SEXTON, G. E. (1982) "The industrial prison: a concept paper." The Prison Journal 62: 13-24.

Vanderbilt Law Review (1970) Special issue on the collateral consequence of a criminal conviction. 23(5).

ABOUT THE AUTHORS

Jack E. Call is Assistant Professor of Criminal Justice at the University of Nebraska at Omaha. He holds a B.S. degree from Ball State University and a J.D. degree from the College of William and Mary. He is completing the requirements for a Ph.D. in political science from the University of Georgia. His professional experience includes service as a legal officer with the U.S. Coast Guard and as Project Director of an LEAA-funded study of Georgia courts.

George H. Cox, Jr. teaches political science and criminal justice at Georgia Southern College. He received a Ph.D. in political science from Emory University in Atlanta. He has specialized in the study of state policy, especially criminal justice and human services policy and was Director of the Office of Research and Evaluation of the Georgia Department of Offender Rehabilitation from 1977 to 1980 and Research Consultant to the Georgia Department of Human Resources from 1980 to 1982. He is the author of a number of papers concerned with the politics of the criminal justice system.

Marc G. Gertz is currently an Associate Professor with the School of Criminology at Florida State University. Dr. Gertz received his Ph.D. in political science from the University of Connecticut in 1976. Dr. Gertz's areas of interest include interest groups and the legislature, the courts, and the role of the social scientist in the courtroom.

Anne M. Heinz, Research Associate at the Center for Urban Affairs and Policy Research at Northwestern University, received her B.A. from Wellesley and M.A. and Ph.D. in Political Science from Northwestern. She has taught at the University of Illinois at Chicago and Barat College and has held research appointments at the University of Chicago Law School and Northwestern. Her research has addressed a number of policy issues in the criminal justice area. She has published articles on innovations in plea bargaining and the legislative politics of criminal law. She is currently a member of the Board of Trustees of the Law and Society Association.

Robert J. Homant received his Ph.D. in clinical psychology from Michigan State University in 1971. After four years as a staff psychologist at the State Prison of Southern Michigan and four years as a chief psychologist at Wisconsin State Prison (Waupun), he joined the staff of the University of Detroit's Criminal Justice Department in 1978. He has published articles in the area of offender rehabilitation, citizen perceptions of police, and the personality of policewomen. He is co-editor with Daniel Kennedy of *Police and Law Enforcement,* published by AMS Press in 1984.

Shannon McIntyre Jordan is Assistant Professor in the Department of Philosophy at George Mason University. Her research interests center on questions related to law and morality, and issues of applied ethics.

Daniel B. Kennedy received his Ph.D. from Wayne State University in 1971. A former probation officer and police academy director, he is currently Associate Professor and Chairman, Department of Criminal Justice, University of Detroit. He has published articles pertaining to clinical sociology, policewomen, and management of stigma. His work has appeared in such journals as *Crime and Delinquency, Journal of Police Science and Administration* and *Journal of Criminal Justice.* He also serves as a visiting lecturer at the FBI Academy, Quantico, Virginia.

Gary N. Keveles is Assistant Professor of Administration of Justice and Research Fellow in the Center for International Studies at the University of Missouri-St. Louis. He is also a Fellow at the Inter-University Seminar on Armed Forces and Society, and affiliated with the International Society for Military Law and Law of War. He received his Ph.D. from the School of Criminal Justice at the University of New York at Albany in 1981. He has conducted research on plea bargaining, sentencing, military justice, and the criminally insane. His current studies include alternatives to prosecution and cross-cultural comparisons of military justice systems.